MANAGING COMMUNICATIONS IN A CRISIS

Managing Communications in a Crisis

Peter Ruff and Khalid Aziz

Gower

© Peter Ruff and Khalid Aziz 2003

All rights reserved. No part of this publication may be reproduced, stored in a retrieval system, or transmitted in any form or by any means, electronic, mechanical, photocopying, recording or otherwise without the permission of the publisher.

Published by
Gower Publishing Limited
Gower House
Croft Road
Aldershot
Hampshire GU11 3HR
England

Gower Publishing Company
Suite 420
101 Cherry Street
Burlington, VT 05401-4405
USA

Peter Ruff and Khalid Aziz have asserted their right under the Copyright, Designs and Patents Act 1988 to be identified as the authors of this work.

British Library Cataloguing in Publication Data

Ruff, Peter
  Managing communications in a crisis
  1. Crisis management 2. Public relations 3. Communication in management 4. Mass media and business
  I. Title II. Aziz, Khalid, 1953-
  658.4' 5

ISBN 0 566 08294 2

Library of Congress Cataloging-in-Publication Data

Ruff, Peter.
  Managing communications in a crisis / Peter Ruff and Khalid Aziz.
    p. cm.
  ISBN 0-566-08294-2
  1. Crisis management. 2. Communication in organizations. 3. Corporations--Public relations.
  I. Aziz, Khalid. II. Title.

HD49.R84 2003
659.2--dc21

2002045233

Typeset in Great Britain by Tradespools, Frome, Somerset
and printed in Great Britain by Antony Rowe Ltd, Chippenham, Wiltshire

Contents

List of figures, examples and case studies		vii
About the authors		ix
Introduction		xi

Part I Understanding Crises and the Theory of Communication

1	Understanding crises	3
2	Elements of crisis management	7
3	Stakeholders and audiences	13
4	Third-party endorsement	21
5	Communications in a crisis	35
6	Science versus emotion	39
7	How the media works	45
8	Single-issue lobby groups	63
9	Lobbying	71
10	The price of failure	77

Part II Practical Crisis Communication

11	Practical steps to prepare for a crisis	87

12	Internal audiences	93
13	The spokesperson	97
14	The crisis team	101
15	Crisis planning and whistle-blowing	107

Part III Appendices

1	The crisis team and crisis centre	115
2	The spokesperson	121
3	Training	125
4	Media handling	127
5	Complaints against the media	131
6	Information technology	137
7	Crisis and the World Wide Web	139
8	County Major Civil Emergency Plan	141
9	Situations	149
10	Crime	157
11	Call centres	167
12	Community groups	169
	Index	171

List of figures, examples and case studies

FIGURES

1.1	Major UK service company list of priorities for crisis management	4
1.2	Crisis news events, United States 1990–98	5
1.3	Sudden versus simmering crises, United States 1997	6
3.1	Internal and external audiences: stakeholders and non-stakeholders	13
13.1	Defence mechanisms in a crisis	99
15.1	Potential hazards checklist	107
15.2	Example section of an impact-minimizing checklist	108

EXAMPLES

3.1	Management performance: Townsend Thorenson	14
3.2	Political performance: the Conservatives and BSE	14
3.3	Financial performance: recoverers and non-recoverers	15
6.1	Train at Victoria Station	40
6.2	The Fresh Fish Test	43
6.3	Rule of Five	43
A4.1	Media log	128
A9.1	The *Marchioness* disaster	152

CASE STUDIES

3.1	Coca-Cola in Belgium in 1999	17
3.2	Pepsi Cola in the United States	18
4.1	Fire in the Channel Tunnel	22
8.1	The environment	65

8.2	Animal rights	66
8.3	The disabled	68
15.1	British Biotech	109

About the authors

PETER RUFF

Peter started his professional journalistic life on a local newspaper, *The Bucks Examiner*, at Chesham in Buckinghamshire. Like most trainee reporters he saw emergency situations at first hand by covering fires, accidents and robberies.

He was one of the first reporters to be recruited into BBC local radio at Brighton in Sussex. He moved to London and, for the next 18 years, worked his way up through posts in radio and television news and current affairs.

In 1983, he was appointed as Moscow correspondent and, over the next four years, covered the East–West arms crises, the shooting down of the South Korean (KAL) airliner and, in 1986, broadcast to the world details of one of the worst nuclear disasters ever, the explosion at the reactor at Chernobyl.

After postings in New York and Washington, he left the BBC to become Director of Communications for a major international waste company which was then encountering criticism from some of the world's leading environmental campaigners.

When he returned to the UK, he took charge of media relations for the chemical industry dealing with environmental crises involving the chemical, oil, pharmaceutical and biotechnology sectors. Through The Aziz Corporation, he advises major FT 250 companies on crisis management communications.

KHALID AZIZ

Khalid spent the first 20 years of his career in the media. Trained by the BBC, he went on to work for a range of news and current affairs programmes from *Newsbeat* on Radio One to *Panorama* on BBC TV.

He presented the BBC programme, *Look North*, which won the Royal Television Society's Regional TV award. Later, in his role as producer and presenter of the TV South business programme, he received the BP Industrial Society TV Industrial Journalist of the Year award. Khalid founded The Aziz Corporation in 1983 and today it is the UK's leading spoken communications consultancy. It has a team of highly experienced practitioners who help senior executives excel at spoken communications. Crisis management is a key element in the company's consultancy portfolio along with other areas of communications such as media handling and presentation skills.

Khalid's tenth book, *Presenting to Win – A Guide for Finance and Business Professionals* was published in 2000.

Introduction

Thanks to the burgeoning information revolution in the latter part of the twentieth century and the start of the new millenium, corporate affairs has come of age. Once known simplistically as 'public relations', it is now a vital and growing discipline within all major companies and organizations.

This book is designed as a three-part guide on how to deal with one key aspect of corporate affairs – crisis management communications. We hope that it will help you develop and tailor your own crisis strategy for your business.

To give some idea how rapidly corporate affairs has developed in recent years, it's worth recalling that, in 1994, a major survey of senior managers in the top UK companies indicated that about 58 per cent of them regarded public relations as worthy of attention. Two years later a similar exercise showed that the figure had risen to 84 per cent and was on an upward path. Today it would be hard to find a senior executive who doesn't have a strong desire to know exactly how his or her organization is communicating and how effectively it is doing so.

The ultimate test of an organization's communication skill is how it deals with a corporate or organizational crisis. It's not difficult to see why: there is an expanding media which is tough on what it regards as management incompetence; shareholders and customers are becoming more demanding; legislation and regulation is being strengthened; and there is greater commercial competition. Thanks to computer networking the communications environment has speeded up and there is now in place the ultimate marketplace for trade and information, the Internet. E-commerce is rapidly changing the way in which business is done.

It varies from one organization to another, but some specialists have estimated that 'reputation' and 'goodwill' can represent as much as 80 per cent of a business's value. Anything that damages these two 'goods' will be very costly indeed.

How do you protect yourself when faced with attacks on your reputation and competence? This book is designed to help you prepare in advance to spot a crisis, deal with it effectively and, crucially, to demonstrate that you have done so. It could, literally, be the factor which keeps you in, or puts you out of, business. As Henry Kissinger once famously remarked: 'An issue ignored is a crisis ensured.'

The pages of this book are littered with real case studies and the lessons to be learnt from them. A major theme is the need to identify areas of risk in advance. We discuss procedures, both managerial and computer-based, to help tackle them efficiently. There are, for example, software programs with 1000 multiple-choice questions for you to ask yourself. If your business scores a total of up to 400 you are probably in a healthy state; 500 and over and you may have to rethink things; 600 and over and you may be heading for big trouble.

Public relations companies, law firms, insurance brokers, banks and a host of other bodies have a stake in saving you and your business. They publish advice and issue crisis management databases, but these are usually from their own perspectives.

We have designed this book to bring many of the strings together and enable you to formulate your own crisis management strategy. In doing so, you will actually see that it is good for business.

Part I

Understanding Crises and the Theory of Communication

1 Understanding crises

There are almost as many definitions as crises themselves but the one which sums it up for us is the following:

> A crisis is any incident or situation, whether real, rumoured or alleged, that can focus negative attention on a company or organization internally, in the media or before key audiences.

In the case of a company that offers shares to the public this means 'anything that could potentially have an impact on the share price'. For other organizations it means 'anything that could actually, or potentially, damage our reputation'.

The use of the word 'potentially' is important here. By far the most satisfying part of our work is helping spot the potential problem or problems and dealing with them before they become a full-blown crisis. The precise nature of an emergency situation might be hard to anticipate but work done in the United States during the 1990s showed that, of all crisis events reported in the media, there were two clear categories: events that were 'simmering' and those that were 'sudden'.

'Sudden' events encompass accidents and emergencies, acts of terrorism, mechanical breakdowns, a hostile take-over or some unexpected legal action.

'Simmering' events cover situations that lurk beneath the organization's surface and can erupt into a crisis at any time. Industrial unrest, criminal actions of varying types and inefficient management would all fall into this category.

An interesting element of companies' and organizations' perspective in crisis management is their general assumption that a crisis will be sudden and unexpected whereas, in reality, it is much more likely to be predictable and expected.

We are retained as crisis management consultants for one of the UK's largest providers of service management for office and residential properties. They operate all over the UK, employ thousands of people and often face emotionally charged situations which, if details reached the media, could have a damaging

UNDERSTANDING CRISES AND THE THEORY OF COMMUNICATION

effect on their share price. For example, a security guard may have allowed robbers into the premises by ignoring procedures, the maintenance of an office central heating system has been inefficient and has led to persistent breakdowns or a waste contractor has been badly chosen and there are complaints from the businesses within the building. On one grizzly occasion, a warden supplied by the company to provide holiday relief at a residential home for the elderly failed to notice that a man had not been seen for a while. It turned out to be ten days, and all that time he had been lying dead from a heart attack in his so-called 'protected' flat.

When, as a direct result of a crisis review, the company called us in to provide advice we asked to see their existing plan. At the front of a very smart manual was a page listing the priorities for crisis management within the company and from where they could expect external criticism if they got it wrong (see Figure 1.1). The interesting thing about that page is that they had the 'sudden' crises at the top of their list of concerns followed by the 'simmering'. Were they correct to do so? We think not.

There is very little accurate data in Britain but, in the United States, the Institute of Crisis Management reviewed thousands of events serious enough to be reported in the media. In all, they looked at 55 000 separate items in 1500 publications between 1990 and 1998. The findings (see Figure 1.2) show quite clearly that 86 per cent of them could be described as 'simmering' and only 14 per cent 'sudden'. For more detailed analysis, they took all the events from one year – 1997 – and broke them down according to the nature of each crisis (see

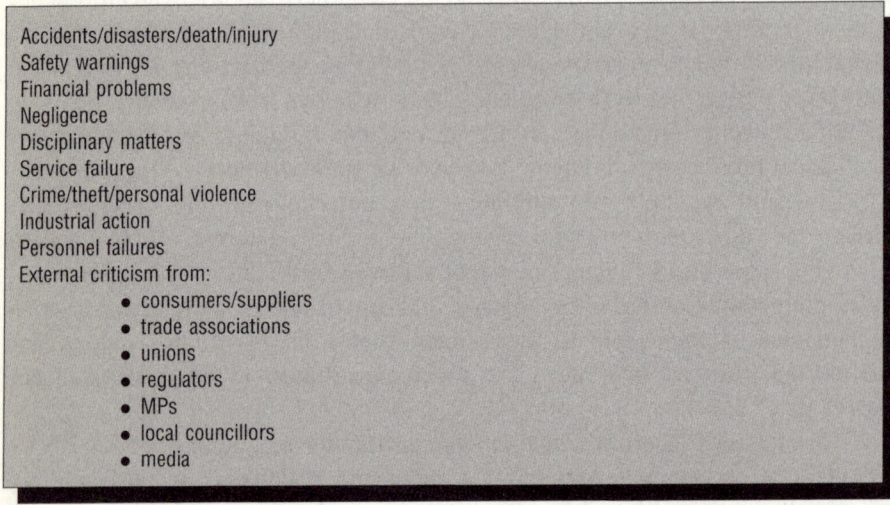

Figure 1.1 Major UK service company list of priorities for crisis management

UNDERSTANDING CRISES

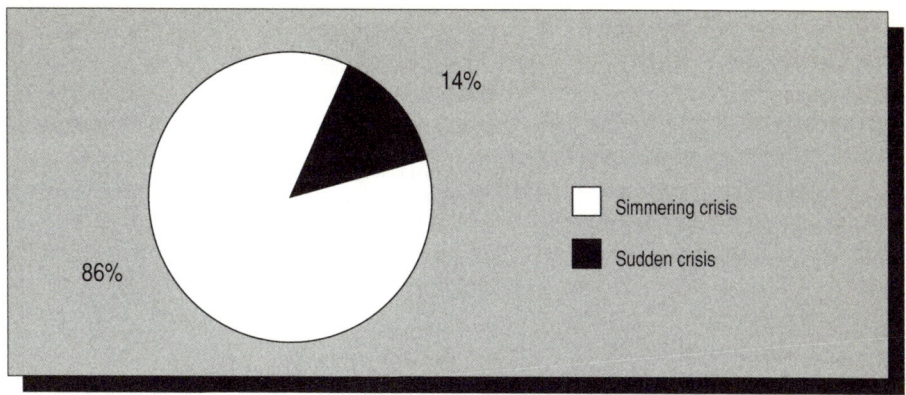

Figure 1.2 Crisis news events, United States 1990–98
Source: United States Institute of Crisis Management.

Figure 1.3). This exercise showed that the majority of the events were 'simmering' and therefore preventable. If you take the top three types of crisis – crime (19 per cent), industrial unrest (18 per cent) and mismanagement (13 per cent) – they add up to half the total of all reported crisis situations and could have been detected and prevented if only there had been such a process in place.

The American business environment may be somewhat different from that in other parts of the world, but we believe that a similar pattern would emerge anywhere. A shrewd crisis management team should be constantly vigilant for 'simmering' issues and have a mechanism in place to prevent them from exploding in the public domain. The evidence in the United States suggests that they should be particularly on the look-out for industrial unrest, mismanagement and 'white-collar' crime!

On the basis that it is possible to counter the vast majority of situations, what about those that we define as 'sudden'? An academic who has studied crisis management over many years, Otto Lerbinger, has identified seven definable types of sudden emergencies. In his book *The Crisis Manager: Facing Risk and Responsibility* (1997) he describes them as follows:

- *Natural disasters*: fires, explosions and bad weather.
- *Technical disasters*: spillages and faulty equipment.
- *Crises of confrontation*: industrial disputes or the development of opposition by single-issue external groups.
- *Acts of malevolence*: terrorism, sabotage and kidnapping.
- *Misplaced management values*: strategic investment errors and ignoring investors' concerns.
- *Acts of deception*: fraud, expenses scams and false invoicing.
- *Management misconduct*: harassment, bribery and corruption.

UNDERSTANDING CRISES AND THE THEORY OF COMMUNICATION

Crime	19%	(usually simmering)
Industrial unrest	18%	(usually simmering)
Mismanagement	13%	(simmering)
Environmental damage		(usually simmering)
Consumer issues		(usually simmering)
Financial damage	12%	(usually simmering)
Sexual harassment		(simmering)
Whistle-blowing		(simmering)
Violence in the workplace		(simmering)
Legal actions	10%	(usually simmering)
Catastrophes	6%	(sudden)
Defects and recalls	6%	(sudden)
Casualty accidents	5%	(sudden)
Racial and sexual discrimination	5%	(simmering)
Hostile take-over	4%	(sudden)
Other	2%	

Note: Within the 'crime' category, what is known as 'white-collar' or management crime (expenses fiddles, fraud, double invoicing and so on) outstripped 'blue-collar crime' (theft, pilfering and damage to goods) by three to one.
Source: United States Institute of Crisis Management.

Figure 1.3 Sudden versus simmering crises, United States 1997

This book is designed to help crisis teams deal with the events that come under these seven categories while recognizing that they are comparatively rare events. We also want to help you identify the more common 'simmering' events and demonstrate how they can be dealt with.

KEY LEARNING POINTS

- A crisis is anything that adversely affects the share price of a company or the reputation of an organization.
- Crises are 'sudden' or 'simmering': the majority 'simmer'.
- Accidents and disasters are rare, but management failures and white-collar crimes are not.

REFERENCE

Lerbinger, Otto (1997), *The Crisis Manager: Facing Risk and Responsibility*, Mahwah, NJ: Lawrence Erlbaum Associates.

2 Elements of crisis management

For both crises that can be spotted in advance and the lesser category that comes out of the blue, there are four stages or elements involved in their management. Your planning must allow for each of these, because only if you deal with each of them successfully will your crisis plan truly work. They cover preparation, notification, communications and recovery. Each will have its own timeline which may cover hours, through days, weeks, months or even years.

THE FOUR ELEMENTS

EMERGENCY PREPAREDNESS

This element is heavily dependent on your business sector and how it is regulated. A sole trader is not expected to prepare for an emergency except by using common sense as a human being. A small business employing a handful of people is expected to take precautions under health and safety and employee regulations. If it is a business dealing in, say, food then other legislation applies. A major manufacturer has to comply with a whole array of health, safety and environmental programmes and must employ teams of people to make sure that they are complied with. A company dealing with potentially dangerous substances such as chemical or nuclear products comes under even tighter regulation that will be enforced by government agencies. Running in parallel with all this, there are often requirements laid down within companies to make sure that their emergency planning is uniform throughout their operations. This is particularly true of corporations with many subsidiaries and a worldwide presence. It is not uncommon for each operating division to have its own plan, but this will have to dovetail with those of the corporate headquarters. Well-run organizations update and practise their emergency preparedness plans at regular intervals.

We will go into more detail in later chapters, but preparedness has to include every aspect of the business you are in. How will an emergency affect personnel, legal, finance, operations, sales, marketing, health and safety, transport and communications?

EMERGENCY NOTIFICATION

If something bad happens, who should be told and how? The notification process is usually divided into what you are obliged to do under the law and legislation and what you should do for the good of your business. Legal obligations are notified by the body responsible for policing the issue and held by the manager tasked with dealing with them. In-house procedures are usually held by the same person but will address corporate standards set by the company itself. They are usually stricter than those laid down by local or national statutes.

The main point is that the company must be aware of both its in-house and external obligations.

Let us take an example of what we mean at the 'high' end of the potential emergency scale. Industries that deal with potentially hazardous materials have statutory obligations under a raft of legislation designed to protect the public. Much of it is covered by UK health, safety and environmental laws but, in recent years, that has extended to European and international regulation as well. Some notification in this category will need to be instant – anyone dealing with nuclear materials, for example, must tell the Nuclear Installations Inspectorate at once. As the emergency unfolds and inquiries are initiated into the cause, other obligations come into play. There will almost certainly be formal procedures for notification within the company. Most crisis plans require the highest officers of the company (that is, those with legal obligations for the welfare of the company, such as board members) to be informed and updated at regular intervals.

It is important to remember that these are formal requirements under company laws and they should not be confused with our next section which covers internal and external crisis communications.

Less formal, but no less important, are notifications that should be made to outside bodies (for example, trade associations) with an interest in your sector. In addition, some contracts with customers and suppliers have clauses that require you to notify them of an emergency that could affect their relationship with you.

One of the best-known notification procedures has been codified by the aviation industry. If the pilots or engineers of an airline encounter something that could endanger air safety they have an obligation to issue a 'bulletin' alerting others. When Concorde crashed in Paris, the operator, Air France, worked closely with their main competitors, British Airways, to identify the cause of the crash, the subsequent explosion and what needed to be reinforced on the aircraft to make it safe to fly again.

Similar arrangements apply to other sectors on the basis that everyone can learn lessons from an emergency. It is also regarded as an important element in the positive public perception of the business.

CRISIS COMMUNICATIONS

This is allied to the section above but involves different disciplines. It involves the 'targeting' in advance of all internal and external audiences and analysing what they will need, and want, to know. It also involves calculating what you want them to know under given circumstances. Many a routine incident or event has been turned into a crisis because too many people were told too much and the situation became exaggerated and out of control.

Control over information is crucial in an emergency but so, too, is the need to give people the power to cascade what information is necessary with speed and efficiency. How often have you read a piece in the newspaper about your company or organization only to realize that you should have been told about it in advance? Media reports are very often the means by which employees find out that their senior manager has walked out or been fired thus throwing the company into chaos.

Of course, security of information is critically important particularly since the advent of instant IT and telecom systems. Part of the preparation for dealing with an emergency is to decide in advance whether you will need secure channels for some information and not others. Remember the civil servant who sent a quick e-mail to her colleagues minutes after the attack on the World Trade Centre in New York? Now, she advised, would be a good moment to get out and 'bury' any negative departmental news. This communication was too 'juicy' to stay secure because it neatly summed up an attitude that was beginning to worry commentators and the public about the government's efforts to manage the news. Consequently, the existence of the e-mail itself became an emergency.

The above example was an internal document that became public unintentionally. In a crisis or emergency it is often a good idea to have draft documents for external audiences prepared in advance so that they only need refining to reflect what has happened. The phrasing of each draft should be worded so as to acknowledge the likely needs of the audience. A draft news release is likely to be substantially different in tone from a letter to a client, although the circumstances and facts may be the same.

CRISIS RECOVERY

Any business or organization that has suffered a physical or reputation crisis has to quickly turn its attention to recovery. As with the three elements already discussed, this involves preparation. Banks and financial institutions will usually make special provision in advance to extend lines of credit in time of crisis, and any reputable insurance company will brief its clients on how to plan for disaster recovery. Items to look out for are the need for physical back-up for lost possessions, processes or buildings. There may also be important issues concerning the restoration of your reputation with external audiences. These may be at the formal, contractual, level involving the breaking of supply contracts with a customer or they may involve the inability to pay suppliers or even what is collectively known as 'goodwill' – the intangible values put on a business relationship. The formal areas can usually be dealt with through the banks and legal processes, but it is in the 'goodwill' areas that special efforts need to be made. Much business is done through 'people buying from people', and it is those relationships that need to be pressed into service if you have suffered a crisis. Across the board of management disciplines there needs to be a mental attitude of 'How do we minimize the damage that has been done to our business or reputation?'. The most obvious example is the supplier–customer relationship. There must be swift communication, for example, between a sales representative and their customer. If the person you are selling to has to rely on the media or other sources for information about your problem, they are likely to become anxious and look for alternative methods of supply. They need to be reassured both in writing and through personal phone calls. External audiences need to know that you are in a period of recovery and that they will receive regular updates about how it is going.

MONITORING AND PREPARATION

Each of the above four elements must be put together using the two vital ingredients for any crisis plan – monitoring and preparation. No emergency plan is going to work unless you keep it regularly under review and, should it ever be implemented, there must be systems to show whether or not it is working.

No emergency plan is going to work unless there are effective early warning systems in place. After all, if you don't know you have a crisis it is very difficult to deal with it!

It is worth remembering, too, that during all crisis situations there is an immediate overload of the communications systems. You must prepare to deal with a much higher volume of two-way telephone conversations, e-mails and face-to-face meetings.

We shall go into greater detail in later chapters, but it is worth remembering that communications run the greatest risk of being the first thing to fail in an emergency and how you handle them may make the difference between whether you are perceived to have coped with the situation successfully or not. It can be extremely frustrating to find that your technical plans for dealing with a problem have worked extremely well but no one seems to have noticed.

Stakeholders, particularly investors, will make their judgements on impressions gained through media coverage. *If you are not credited with having dealt with a situation effectively, then you haven't.* They will also base their future actions on whether they felt that you were open and honest. An investor is unlikely to keep their money in a company that does not appear to be able to confidently handle the unexpected. Your response to crisis will be seen as a direct reflection of how you operate on a day-to-day basis.

There can have been few crises more devastating in recent years than the terrorist attacks in New York and Washington in September 2001. Mayors of New York often have to deal with emergencies, and Rudi Guiliani seized the moment by being seen to be in charge. He was honest about the situation at the World Trade Centre and apparently tireless in trying to recover the situation. It could be argued that he almost turned it into a celebration of New York.

In Washington, no one seemed to be in charge and the public perception was of a nation's capital in chaos. This situation was not helped a few weeks later when there was a terrorist scare involving anthrax and half the Congress disappeared in panic.

One sure way of avoiding such public perceptions and being in control is to have made preparations in advance for how you will communicate. This is easier than many people appreciate due to the fact that there are rarely more than three new features in a crisis:

- What happened?
- How did it happen?
- Whose fault was it?

Most of the remaining information is background and can be prepared in advance.

We recommend that the crisis team ask themselves a series of questions about how the organization does what it does. Better still, they should get an outside opinion on how that same information comes across. Insiders take too much for granted and are less likely to pose difficult questions in a time of crisis.

Finally, this chapter ends with three quotations for those of you who either know you should have a crisis plan but have put off doing it or have been told not to bother because 'it's not a priority'.

> News is what someone, somewhere wants to suppress; the rest is advertising. (Lord Northcliffe, newspaper proprietor)

> Bad news travels fast and sells best. (Anonymous)

> In a crisis you are the only ones looking after your interests. (Peter Ruff and Khalid Aziz)

LEARNING POINTS

- ◆ There are four elements to a crisis – preparation, notification, communication and recovery.
- ◆ You must have an early warning system that works.
- ◆ You must monitor what is being done and said because public perception of how successful you are is vital.
- ◆ Bad news travels fast and sells best.

3 Stakeholders and audiences

When a sudden event occurs there will be no time to identify all the people who need to be informed about what happened, how it happened and what is being done about it.

It is a crucial part of the crisis team's role to keep updated lists of internal and external audiences who may need to be informed and dealt with. Much will depend on the scale of the business or the size of the organization but, generally, there are concentric circles of audiences (some overlapping and some not). Audiences fall into two definable categories: stakeholders and non-stakeholders (see Figure 3.1).

Each sector has a different level of involvement and how you address their concerns during a crisis is an important part of the planning process. You will have to decide in advance, for example, how your receptionists, telephonists and others will filter calls from each category. You will also have to decide who will deal with the concerns of each caller or e-mailer since there may be a high level of emotions involved. One good way of thinking this issue through in advance is to ask the question: 'If we fail to deal with this person's concerns what could be the consequences?'

Figure 3.1 Internal and external audiences: stakeholders and non-stakeholders

Some audiences will need a concise, but high-level, briefing accompanied by assurances that a more detailed explanation will, be forthcoming when the emergency is over. Suppliers, customers, regulators and local authorities would fall into that camp. Others, such as off-duty staff or relatives, will need immediate information and reassurances from the human resources department.

The most demanding external audience is likely to be the media. They will need immediate information from a trained spokesperson not only on what may have happened but also on the background of the company or organization.

Why is it important to take this trouble in advance? Simply because it is the way in which you treat these audiences before, during and after an emergency that might have a crucial impact on whether or not you remain in business. If you are perceived by these audiences to have handled things well, then you survive. If not, you don't. The following examples illustrate this point.

> **EXAMPLE 3.1**
>
> **Management performance: Townsend Thorenson**
>
> Townsend Thorenson was one of the leading companies in the cross-Channel ferry business between Britain and Europe. They had a slick marketing and advertising operation and carried thousands of passengers and vehicles every year.
>
> Then came the *Zeebrugge* tragedy caused by one of their ships leaving harbour with its main door partly open and resulting in great loss of life and a massive media coverage which focused on shortcomings in the way the company operated its ferries. Staff morale and training were at a low level, and it emerged that safety measures were often ignored in the rush to turn around the ships.
>
> As so often happens, companies with this kind of profile are usually unprepared for a crisis and, not surprisingly, the management responded to the event in an ill-considered and chaotic way, thereby losing the confidence of crucial external audiences and stakeholders.
>
> Not only did the top management lose their jobs, but the company eventually disappeared altogether. Its assets were taken over by a competitor and the brand name totally disappeared.

> **EXAMPLE 3.2**
>
> **Political performance: the Conservatives and BSE**
>
> At the political level it could be argued that elections are won or lost according to the confidence, or lack of it, expressed by audiences. Observers have ascribed the defeat of the Conservative government

STAKEHOLDERS AND AUDIENCES

in 1997 to a loss of credibility in the way in which it dealt with crises. One of the largest of these was the BSE crisis involving beef cattle.

The government was perceived to be uncertain about the issue and initially denied that there was a problem.

When that position became unsustainable, they appeared to panic and seemed to be making policy on an ad hoc basis. As a result, the audiences (voters and the opposition parties in particular) and stakeholders (farmers, the meat industry and other members of the food processing and distribution industry) lost millions of pounds and saw a drop in public confidence in the UK beef industry.

When audiences in other European countries became involved, the issue developed into an international crisis as well.

EXAMPLE 3.3
Financial performance: recoverers and non-recoverers

Putting a financial cost on crisis management is difficult because it almost always involves a company's non-profit sector activity (communications, human resources and the law), and its effectiveness is hard to quantify.

In their 1996 book *The Impact of Catastrophes on Shareholder Value*, researchers Rory Knight and Deborah Pretty demonstrated the financial vulnerability of companies when they face a crisis. After studying 15 incidents involving disasters affecting major international businesses, they came to the conclusion that there is a direct co-relation between the way in which each company handles the situation and its financial future.

There are, in effect, those who 'recover' and those who do not. Yet, recovery was not a simple matter of whether or not the business had invested in catastrophe insurance to provide financial compensation. Rather, the company's financial viability was heavily influenced by the perceptions of stakeholders and other audiences. If these groups thought that the management had performed well under pressure, then they kept their investments in the company; if not, they sold shares resulting in the company's devaluation.

In other words, a crisis puts an instant spotlight on whether the business can cope or not.

NON-RECOVERERS

Knight's and Pretty's analysis showed that the international chemical manufacturer Union Carbide never did recover its stock price following the explosion at Bhopal in India in 1994. The incident caused 3000 deaths and many more injuries, and the company lost at least $527 million in revenue. In addition, the management was perceived to be heartless in the way it dealt with the victims and the Indian government. It haggled with the government over compensation, leading the media, politicians and others to believe that the company was more concerned with financial losses than with human suffering. There was also the perception that, because the disaster occurred in a developing country and affected relatively poor people, the company thought that it could get away with paying less than it would have to in an advanced Western country.

Similarly, when the oil tanker *Exxon Valdez* ran aground and polluted the Alaskan coast in 1989, the company lost billions of dollars and its share price never recovered. This happened because the management was thought to be trying to keep a low profile in the light of allegations that they had employed a drunken captain. They were also seen to be negligent about keeping oil pollution countermeasures up-to-date and in good working order. Much of the management's attitude was dictated by legal advice that any comment admitting mistakes would only add to the financial legal liability. There seems little doubt today that the negative impact on its balance sheet caused by attacks on its reputation was a far more serious issue than the compensation payments the company made in Alaska.

RECOVERERS

In 1988 a terrorist bomb brought down Pan-Am flight 103 at Lockerbie in Scotland causing 270 deaths and a financial loss of $652 million. In this case, the stock price did recover because it was seen as an act of terrorism and not management failure. There was talk of a lack of security but this was directed against airports and government agencies and not purely the airline.

It is ironic that Pan-Am did go out of business eventually. It had been showing signs of financial fragility before the crash but it was a reluctance on the part of passengers to travel on Pan-Am afterwards, not the way in which it had handled the crisis, that tipped the balance.

A complete recovery was registered by another company that was the victim of terrorism. An IRA bomb went off immediately outside one of Commercial Union Insurance main offices in the City of London in 1992. As an insurance company, with a professional interest in risk assessment and recovery, it immediately activated a well-prepared crisis plan and had alternative premises up and running

> by the following week. There were three deaths and many other injuries. The financial loss was calculated at $2170 million, but there was a total recovery of the share price.

It seems only sensible, then, for all organizations to have a plan for how they would cope with a crisis. It is our belief that corporate governance issues – including how management identifies, manages and eliminates risk – will feature heavily in future annual reports. It will become as familiar as the financial statement and balance sheet, the former often heavily influencing the latter.

A crisis communications strategy that forms a part of the technical crisis plan can only be effective with stakeholders and other audiences if the messages are plausible, believable and have the manifest backing of senior management. It is that management, after all, that has the most to lose, particularly if it has expansion plans or global ambitions. A half-hearted approach by senior management will be seen as weakness or an attempt to evade responsibilities.

The following two case studies show how company performance can be influenced by stakeholder and audience reaction.

> **CASE STUDY 3.1**
> **Coca-Cola in Belgium in 1999**
> The Coca-Cola corporation, based in Atlanta in the United States, has a market capitalization of about £160 billion and is one of the world's leading 'brands'.
>
> When it was faced with a major threat to its 'brand image' in 1999 it did not appear to be prepared to act swiftly or effectively. That failure had a negative impact on its key stakeholders and audiences, and the stock price consequently plunged. That, in turn, led to the resignation of a number of board members including the American chief executive.
>
> The chain of events started when the Belgium government discovered that some bottles of Coca-Cola had become slightly contaminated with chemicals that could cause cancer. The government initially decided to keep quiet but, when the news leaked, the prime minister was forced to resign and there was a major recall of Coca-Cola products in Belgium, France and other European markets.
>
> As the situation continued to unravel, a dozen executives from America (led by the vice-president of Global Communications) were despatched to sort things out.
>
> At first, they acted defensively, claiming that there was no threat to human health and suggesting that it could be a case of 'mass

UNDERSTANDING CRISES AND THE THEORY OF COMMUNICATION

hysteria'. It soon became clear that their key audience – Coca-Cola drinkers – did not believe them and stopped buying the product. Politicians, another key audience for an international company, reacted negatively because it represented more clear evidence that the public was sensitive to anything involving food chain contamination issues.

The incident demonstrated that throwing an all-American crisis team into a sensitive European issue was not enough. They failed to appreciate the seriousness of the matter and misjudged the reaction of audiences and stakeholders.

CASE STUDY 3.2
Pepsi Cola in the United States
What started as a few unconfirmed reports that cans of Diet Pepsi had been tampered with in one city turned into a flood of complaints from all over the United States.

Pepsi immediately ordered an investigation by outside experts who found that the claims were false. As a result, the company launched a major and high-profile rebuttal proving that tampering could not have occurred. Video news releases were despatched. The CEO was interviewed and a commissioner from the Food and Drug Administration backed up the company's claim that it was the victim of a widespread campaign by people wanting to get financial compensation for a non-existent threat.

What the company had done was to define the risk to customers, distributors and other stakeholders. They also acted swiftly to find out the facts and then demonstrated responsible management action. As a result, Pepsi avoided a costly recall, limited the loss of market share for their products and increased consumer confidence by showing a high level of concern for safety.

Most important of all, the company crisis team had prepared for such an eventuality in advance.

LEARNING POINTS

- Identify key audiences in advance.
- Audiences are divided into stakeholders and non-stakeholders.

- Plan how you will deal with their concerns – how you treat them may decide the future of your organization.
- Some companies recover financially; others do not.
- It is crucial for management to be seen to have done well.
- The management must assure investors that plans are in place.
- Do not rely on communications alone; a technical plan is the first priority.
- Do not underestimate the potential global impact of a 'local' event.
- Messages must be confident and believable.

REFERENCE

Knight, Rory and Pretty, Deborah (1996), *The Impact of Catastrophe on Shareholder Value*, Oxford Executive Research Briefing, Oxford; Templeton College.

4 Third-party endorsement

While it is important to plan in advance how to deal with internal and external audiences in a crisis, there is another group that needs to be considered should things suddenly go wrong – organizations or individuals who have no direct financial or other interest in your business but who can be relied on to say good things about you or support what you say.

They are collectively known as 'third-party endorsees', and it is a key part of crisis planning to identify, in advance, those non-stakeholders who would be prepared to speak on your behalf if asked to do so by the media or others.

Part of your crisis preparation, and good business practice, is to make sure that these people know as much as possible about your operations, your good management and the preparations you have made to deal with trouble. They should not be one-off contacts but people who are regularly briefed about what is going on.

It is impossible to publish a fully comprehensive list of third-party endorsees but some fall into obvious categories depending on what business you are in and the type of crisis you are dealing with.

THE EMERGENCY SERVICES

In almost any business it is worth keeping in touch with the emergency services if only to regularly check your office security measures or fire precautions. In the case of continuous production factories and companies dealing with hazardous materials it is mandatory that you regularly test procedures with the emergency services – the more often the better – since personnel on both sides change and it is good to have personal contact. Drills based on potentially real scenarios can be practised and essential feedback can be received from all those involved.

Just how many services will be involved is heavily dependent on the site and the potential emergency. Some participants are more obvious than others. The police, fire brigade and ambulance service are involved in almost all sudden emergency situations, whether they are actually needed or not. An emergency in a high-profile manufacturing plant, a hotel, an airport or any other public building will trigger an automatic response from all these services in case they are required. It is not unknown to have seven fire engines arrive to deal with a small kitchen fire if it is in a hospital, an old people's residence or a high-rise tower block.

Other emergency services are less obvious but often just as important. Water, gas, electricity and telephone companies all have emergency teams on standby 24 hours a day and will often be first on the scene so that they can cut supplies to enable the other emergency service personnel to work in safety.

In addition, other instant response groups from organizations such as the Salvation Army (to provide clothing and shelter), the Red Cross, the local authority, the Highways Agency, the Environment Agency and government health, safety and environment departments may all need to be involved or informed.

If there is any chance of environmental hazard there are specialist round-the-clock advisory services set up by specialist sectors such as chemical manufacturers and transporters and the oil and pharmaceutical providers.

If there is any chance of pollution to the air, land or water then the Weather Bureau will be instantly notified and asked for advice on expected weather conditions. This can be crucial if there is a sudden toxic emission from a plant. Only the weather service will know exactly where and how strongly the wind is blowing!

If there is a crisis at sea it will almost certainly be coordinated by the Coastguard Service and involve various, often voluntary, units from the Royal National Lifeboat Institution, inshore rescue and specialist diving teams. The latter are often provided by the military as, of course, are the various branches of Air Sea Rescue.

When you are trying to second-guess a crisis scenario that may affect your organization, ask yourself: 'If someone from one of those agencies was asked is XYZ company a good one, is it safety-conscious and do they handle things well, will they say "yes"?' The following Channel Tunnel case study is a good example.

> **CASE STUDY 4.1**
> **Fire in the Channel Tunnel**
> The UK operators of the Channel Tunnel developed extensive crisis management plans along with their counterpart project managers in France. Apart from special considerations such as terrorism, sabotage, smuggling, illegal immigration or structural failure of the

tunnel itself, the most obvious crisis would be a fire, explosion or accident – particularly one occurring at the midway point.

That, of course, is exactly what happened.

Mercifully there was no loss of life but the company's reputation was badly damaged on the issue of third-party endorsement. In an incident like this it is vital that the emergency services comment on how efficiently the tunnel authority had put the crisis plan into action and that everyone had worked well to deal with the problem. However, no such endorsement was forthcoming.

Instead, the fire brigade in Kent and the French went on record as saying that they had long warned that such an incident could occur if the company insisted on using special open-sided rail wagons to transport freight lorries through the tunnel.

Even worse, the head of the Kent fire brigade had given an interview to the BBC some months beforehand and, in it, had spelt out his fears about a fire breaking out inside the tunnel. His video was quickly found in the archive, dusted down and replayed regularly during the reporting of the incident.

There was another crisis management twist to the Channel Tunnel fire. Despite the savagery of the blaze, the company insisted that all would be well and that the tunnel would reopen for business within a matter of days. Those days swiftly lengthened into weeks and then into months resulting in a devaluation of the credibility of everything the company subsequently said about the situation.

Why did the company do this?

The answer is horribly simple. For years, the tunnel company had been losing money and was heavily in debt to scores of international banks. The last thing they wanted was for potential customers to cash in their tunnel tickets and switch them to the sea ferries. In effect, they reached for the crisis plan that told their spokespeople to be reassuring about the reopening time. In the event, it had the opposite effect and helped to portray the company as being hopelessly out of control.

The model answer to any enquiry about reopening after an accident is: 'We will only resume business when we are sure that it is safe to do so.'

A major crisis management lesson: if potential third-party endorsees appear to be shaky, identify the problem and neutralize it in advance. Also, try to reach for the most appropriate crisis plan.

It is also worth remembering that, under some circumstances, the job of communicating with the public and other audiences is designated to the emergency services by statute. They might, for example, want to take sole charge of briefing the media and public service announcements. However, do not necessarily be fooled into agreeing. It sounds logical and public-spirited but can cause you a lot of damage. Remember that one of the first rules of crisis management is that you should be in control of the flow of information about your company or organization if something has gone wrong because *you must be seen to be in charge*. A police or fire officer cannot possibly do that for you. Their audiences are often different. Cynics would say that most fire crews want to be perceived as heroic and will exaggerate the seriousness of an incident. They, after all, always want more fire engines, helicopters and other specialist equipment so it is in their interest, but not yours, to make an emergency call-out sound worse than it actually is.

It must be said, however, that police officers of all types are more cautious in what they say to outsiders, including the media. This is because they are trained in the rules of giving evidence and, also, there may be criminal or civil court proceedings to come. Nevertheless, it is still not beyond them to whisper behind their hands words to the effect that 'it was an accident waiting to happen'!

Wherever possible, make sure that anyone in this category speaks about you as being a responsible company and one that has always been fully cooperative with the emergency services in terms of regularly training and practising for emergencies.

MEDICAL ISSUES

Most organizations have trained medical practitioners ranging from a full-time doctor who heads a team of nurses and other auxiliary staff in a major company to qualified first-aiders in small offices. Companies that specialize in medical products or pharmaceuticals also obviously employ medical specialists, and continuous process industries often employ occupational therapists and people specializing in health, safety and environmental issues.

A sudden emergency or crisis may well involve a medical element where their expertise will come to the fore. Other similar situations might be a product recall involving a health and safety issue, the failure of a drug under test and so on.

Can these people legitimately be called third-party endorsees? Clearly not – because they work for the organization and will be perceived by outside audiences to be partisan, despite any ethics training they may have done. History is littered with examples of medical experts working for companies, who have proved to be completely unreliable in their judgement about a health issue involving their employers. Any crisis planning involving health issues must include the identification of people who can speak reliably and credibly on your behalf. They must be experts in the products you make or the pollutants you have to deal with.

In the case of companies that manufacture medical products this is often easily dealt with by calling on the officials who clear them for sale to the public. In the case of drugs, this is now the aptly named NICE – the National Institute for Clinical Excellence. Other organizations specialize in medical equipment of all sorts, and there are specialist units that deal with industrial ailments and environmental impact issues.

If a crisis occurs that may involve the need for third-party endorsement of what you do, it is a good idea to have already clearly identified who will comment in your favour so that you can steer journalists and other interested parties towards them.

Don't just stop at regulatory bodies. The local GP near your plant or office can be useful, as can university professors who study medical issues relating to your products. Specialist hospital consultants are another avenue of endorsement. However, they can only be effective on your behalf if they are fully briefed on issues in advance. You need to carry on a continuous dialogue with them in anticipation of the unlikely event of a medical-based crisis.

Another possibility is that you may well find yourself facing an implacable scientific enemy – for example, someone who is convinced that your activities or products are a threat to health or a group that will seize every opportunity to criticize what you do and how you do it. If you find yourself confronted with this situation, take the trouble to note who they are and try to engage them. This strategy might involve substantial amounts of management time, finance and effort but it can often be worth it.

The international food manufacturer, Nestlé is a classic case. For years it suffered from negative publicity generated by powerful lobby groups that criticized their marketing of baby foods, particularly powdered milk, to families in the developing world. At first, the company appeared to dismiss the highly detailed scientific claims as being the work of food campaign activists who were opposed to international capitalism.

That did not work.

The company then decided that it would be more beneficial to try to engage the campaigners. This took many months but, eventually, even the most vociferous opponents were won over. One group even issued a statement agreeing to back the Nestlé position.

Years of negative coverage were replaced by a period of comparative calm because now, if there is doubt about the products and how they are marketed, they can call on their former enemies as third-party endorsees.

However, the company cannot sit on its laurels. New groups have been formed on the baby milk issue and they are mounting new publicity campaigns all the time.

The testing of animals by the drug and cosmetic companies has been a particularly virulent issue. One major consumer goods manufacturer we worked with found that animal rights activists were suggesting that the company was persistently testing on animals. However, they had in fact taken the decision many years beforehand to stop testing, not least because the majority of their staff were against it.

On the basis that anything negative that could hit the stock price – whether or not true – constitutes a crisis, the company instigated a proactive campaign to show how responsible it had been. It even conducted a public relations audit from country to country to make sure that its own managers knew what the company policy was. Finding, to its horror, that many of their people were utterly ignorant of the details, it organized workshops so that the media could be accurately briefed

Eventually the activists backed down and issued statements in support of the company position and praising its social responsibility. Again, engagement proved to be effective and a third-party endorsee was recruited.

Medical and health issues like this are a particularly complex element in crisis management mainly because they are often highly scientific subjects that are only marginally understood by those outside. It is not enough to say that you are doing a good, safe job as the response will be: 'They would say that, wouldn't they?' Get third parties to back you up.

PRODUCT ISSUES

These generally fall into two types of crisis: the recall of items because something has affected the production design or process or there has been contamination; and product tampering, often carried out by a disgruntled employee or by someone outside the company who is trying to threaten the producer or retailer.

With product recall the golden rule is to be open, honest and truthful. Be seen to be acting swiftly and decisively and spend whatever it takes to make sure that suppliers, distributors, retailers and customers are warned. This can be done through press releases, advertising, media interviews or a combination of all three. Here too, it is wise to have a third-party endorsee available to speak on your behalf about how much care is taken to make sure the goods produced are safe for sale.

If advertising is required, make sure that the media journalists sing your praises for acting in the interests of customers rather than your own profit margins.

It is often tempting to limit a recall because you think that the problem is confined to a particular batch. If you are certain, fair enough. If you are not 100 per cent sure, then opt for a total recall. The follow-up is also crucial. If enquiries illuminate exactly what went wrong, make sure that you are seen to be alerting other companies who could encounter a similar situation. Be seen to be campaigning, if necessary, for packaging changes or production-line modernization.

Product tampering is an altogether trickier issue since it will almost certainly involve someone who is committing a crime. Involve the police and others at the earliest possible opportunity. This way, they will turn out to be your best third-party endorsement if everything goes well.

For manufacturers under these circumstances there is a potential problem in that it may take some time for your best efforts and cooperation with the authorities to be recognized. The tamperer may well have blackmail in mind, and the police may find it necessary to impose a news black-out on the issue. This is done with the full support of the media. But their support is contingent on one condition – that, when the culprit or culprits are caught, they are given full and unexpurgated details of how the drama unfolded. Since arrests usually lead to criminal charges, there will be a further delay before the court case is resolved. If a guilty verdict is passed, all the details can be published. At this point, third-parties can be wheeled out to praise your cooperation and responsibility, and the subsequent publicity should be broadly positive.

If, however, the verdict is 'not guilty' you have a dilemma – to say nothing at all or cooperate with the media who still have a good story but cannot say that it is pegged to a criminal trial. Ultimately, you could end up by appearing to be the culprit for not making tamper-proof products!

These are fine judgements that should be made after seeking careful legal advice but, generally speaking, our advice is to cooperate as much as possible. Always have people on hand who can endorse your positions.

STAFFING ISSUES

These usually involve redundancies, industrial action or a combination of both. In recent years sexual and racial harassment have also come into play, along with 'unfair dismissal'.

Whatever the circumstances, your reputation as an employer will be on the line and it is here that you can reap the benefit of a good reputation or the whirlwind of a bad one.

If you detect a 'simmering' problem of this nature make sure that you identify all potential sources of third-party endorsement. Try to enlist trade union support, if at all possible, as well as officials who may have been involved in reconciliation or human resource consultants. It may also be useful to identify other employers who face similar situations. Certainly, the Confederation of British Industry, the Institute of Directors and the Business Link network all have experts in employment law who can be approached for advice and support.

You will almost certainly require legal support. Make sure that the lawyers you select are experts in the field and can act as a third party on the general principles at stake despite the fact that they are directly engaged by you. There are often complex staffing issues to be resolved and one will almost certainly be whether you try to 'gag' them for the duration of the unrest or while the issue is being resolved. In our experience, this approach nearly always fails and is counterproductive. Nevertheless, staff should be encouraged to undertake interviews with the media in their own time rather than yours!

Since the strike-laden 1970s and 1980s, many more companies have been including union representatives or works councils discussions about strategic decisions. If you can obtain positive endorsement for your actions from the people you employ, so much the better.

In 1999, the BMW company told the Rover Group at Longbridge that significant redundancies would have to be made if the plant was to survive. On the morning of the announcement, spokespeople from BMW and Rover gave interviews to the media justifying their action. Nothing odd about that, except that they were then joined by the key union convenor who said that he and his members had been fully included in the talks over the previous year and were agreed that the lay-offs were the only option.

BMW's subsequent disposal of the Rover Group and the haggling over who would take over ownership should not obscure the fact that, at the time, the company obtained clear (though not strictly 'third-party') endorsement for its actions.

The episode illustrated that the Rover management was caring, inclusive and honest in its approach to its employees.

FINANCIAL ISSUES

There are so many crisis scenarios that could fit into this category that it is impossible to list them all. Suffice it to say that they range from a major event such as a hostile take-over being launched against you through to significant trade losses down to relatively minor financial irregularities that could lead to a severe crisis.

Whatever the severity of the scenario, it is the way in which your management copes with the situation that could make the difference between your organization's survival or demise.

A financial crisis is complicated by the fact that you have internal financial support, usually reporting to the finance director, and an array of outside consultants who are hired by you but can also be seen as third parties. Investment houses, bankers, auditors, insurance companies and solicitors are independent of you, but each has a strong interest in your financial well-being.

There are also other categories of financial observers who are not directly connected to you but will always be available for comment on your financial health. Financial analysts who track the fortunes of publicly owned companies are always ready to advertise their own expertise by briefing journalists and investors on how they think a company is being managed.

In crisis management communications the trick is to try to ensure that what your in-house team is saying is echoed by the 'retained' third parties and those who are not tied to you in any kind of formal sense. Most companies go to great lengths to make sure that analysts are regularly briefed about past performance and future strategy. If they are good at this, they will also make sure that the key messages, if not the technical detail, dovetail with what other interested parties, particularly the media, are being told.

Remember, though, that there has to be *de facto* honesty involved in all this. The corporate world is littered with examples of companies who have been brought to their knees by executives who have tried to mislead even their own advisers.

In the world of auditing who can forget the Robert Maxwell pension scandal? A whole raft of advisers were misled into thinking that the company was in better financial shape than it actually was. The accountants charged with auditing the numbers chose to believe rather too much of what the company directors and accountants were telling them. As a result, they ended up paying out millions of pounds in compensation to Mirror Group pensioners when it was revealed how little they had probed. Having said that, how tempting it must be to keep quiet when you know that, if you blow the whistle, you may lose the business to one of your competitors.

A financial crisis makes it imperative that what the company says is underwritten by its own advisers. Transparency and a willingness to face the most unpleasant of facts are crucial.

Quite often, bankers and investment fund managers step into a crisis situation themselves. If they believe that the issue is not being handled well, they may even insist on top management changes and the installation of outside non-executive directors if they feel that their investments are being put in jeopardy.

If you are planning how you would deal with a financial crisis it is useful to assess the potential damage of certain actions. For example, directors are often tempted to sell shares when they know that their company is going to go through a bad patch. How is that going to be perceived by the company's investors and third-party endorsees? While the reasons for share selling may be completely above board, it can also be a signal to the financial markets that all is not well.

A financial crisis can often be triggered by a management situation that has not been handled correctly. For years, the retail group, Marks and Spencer, relaxed in the knowledge that it was at the top of the tree in terms of customer satisfaction and the quality of its goods and services. It was led by a powerful chairman, Sir Richard Greenbury, who was also the chief executive. The business was characterized by a strong hierarchical approach and, crucially, the senior management would never deal with journalists or other outsiders who they considered to be negative about the merits of the great 'M and S'.

Things began to unravel and approach crisis when the issue of whether Sir Richard should split his roles and prepare for his successor to take over turned into a boardroom struggle. The details began to leak into the media and, just when the store chain needed as much third-party endorsement as possible, it faced some of the most hostile coverage a company has ever had.

Journalists approached customers and suppliers and found a uniformly negative approach to the way in which the company was being run. Suppliers said that M and S buyers treated them with contempt. Customers said the clothes were no longer fashionable. Other stores said that the company operated in an old-fashioned and wasteful manner. Financial analysts said that the share price of the company valued it as less than the total of its fixed assets.

For years, the firm lurched from crisis to crisis. Management came and went. The identity of the stores was revamped and some of its international businesses were sold off.

By 2002, Marks and Spencer seemed to to have turned the corner and now third-party endorsees are beginning to say nice things about them again. It was very much a case of a financial decline triggered by the failure to tackle structural management errors rather than by the performance of the stores themselves.

ENVIRONMENTAL ISSUES

It is difficult to put a precise date on it but, by our calculation, environmental issues began to emerge as important considerations for management crisis-handling from the mid-1970s. The reasons for this are too complex to go into here but, in our opinion, there were two principal factors at work: academic research, which led to books such as *Silent Spring* which highlighted the need for the developed world to take more responsibility for the environment; and, more or less concurrently, several spectacular environmental disasters (for example, Three Mile Island, Flixborough) that raised questions as to whether industry was doing enough to prevent pollution.

Highly organized and well-financed campaigning groups began to be established worldwide with the aim of highlighting manmade threats to the environment. Furthermore, publicity stunts and well-researched allegations by organizations such as Greenpeace, Friends of the Earth and the Sierra Club began to have an impact on the reputation of governments, companies and other organizations that were perceived to be indifferent to the impact their activities might be having on the environment.

It was a wake-up call. In future, public opinion would have to be accommodated on this issue like never before.

The campaign groups became skilled at attracting attention to issues that had hitherto been the stuff of academic papers and scientific journals. Consequently, tabloid newspapers began to highlight the plight of the whale and the tuna. Landfill sites and waste incinerators were featured in television 'exposé' documentaries. Spectacular 'raids' were carried out on the premises of companies or organizations that had been deemed to be harming the environment by their activities.

The campaigners were quick to seize their opportunities; businesses and governments were slow to react. As a result, so-called Green movements began to have some success in public opinion polls and elections and, eventually, business was compelled to respond. From the office manager concerned about how to recycle paper through to the managing director who had to decide whether to accept delivery of a petrol-guzzling company car, the environment was firmly on the agenda.

Interestingly, many companies and organizations found themselves under pressure from their own staff to make changes in how they did business. Other stakeholders such as customers, suppliers and shareholders began to build environmental factors into their judgements about who they did business with.

In crisis management communications terms the environment became a hot issue. Egged on by politicians who had come under pressure from their constituents, regulators began to tighten environmental codes and the media began to hunt for violators who could be exposed. There were plenty to be found.

When faced with allegations of bad environmental practice company managements often go into denial and are hurt when their records are attacked. They say things like 'We always operate within our consent levels', meaning that they do not discharge more effluent into the air or water than permitted by regulations.

Others, including the general public, environmental groups and the media, see things quite differently. For 'consent' they read 'licence to pollute'. They do not understand, and will not tolerate, the notion that, often, wealthy companies are allowed to flush away their industrial waste without paying for it.

Your environmental crisis communications planning must be sensitive to the fact that you might have to explain complicated industrial processes and their impact on the environment to external audiences who are unsympathetic. Messages and announcements must address the emotion behind the issues and not simply hope that the issues themselves will just go away, like pollution.

The Shell oil company, which wanted to sink Brent Spar, one of its old North Sea platforms, as a way of decommissioning it, found out how true this was.

At first the company's instincts were perfectly correct. It sought, and obtained, scientific advice on how best to get rid of the platform. Knowing that it would be a contentious issue, it was looking for the most cost-effective and environmentally safe way of dealing with it. The answer came back that the best solution was to tow it to a deep part of the North Sea and sink it.

It was at this point that the company made a fatal error. Because the scientific opinion was so conclusive, it announced the burial at sea with little or no thought about the reaction of environmentalists, the media and politicians. A thunderstorm broke over the company's head and, despite its best efforts to remedy matters, the public relations situation was so negative that the parent company in Holland ordered the UK management team to reverse its decision. The sheer weight of public opinion and the subsequent boycotting of Shell products made it impossible to stick with the original option for dealing with the platform.

To be totally fair, the environmental group, Greenpeace, which led the campaign against Shell, created their own crisis. They made claims about the quantity of oil still in the platform and suggested, wrongly, that the contents would be sunk as well. Subsequently, they were quick to apologize but briefed the press that their error was not enough to destroy their overall case about Brent Spar, shrewdly using the occasion of its *mea culpa* to ram home the basic message. 'How', they asked, 'is it possible for a hugely rich oil company to stick drilling platforms into the North Sea but make no proper financial provision for disposal?'

This was a damaging episode for an organization that prides itself on its scientific research, but the harm done to Shell's finances and reputation was much worse.

LEARNING POINTS

- Try to identify all issues that might require third-party endorsement.
- Select and cultivate all third-party endorsees.
- Do not hand too much power over communications to the emergency services or others.
- In medical matters, outside support is crucial.
- Try to enter into dialogue, even with 'enemies'.
- If product recall is the issue, be swift, honest and open.
- Be seen to be part of the solution and not part of the problem.
- Try to get trade union endorsement for employee-related issues.
- In a financial crisis, there are in-house, consultancy and third-party messages – they must all dovetail.
- On environmental issues, think it through from the public perspective.

5 Communications in a crisis

UNCOVERING POTENTIAL CRISES

Having established what a crisis is and taken steps to neutralize its potential effects, let us look at methods of finding out what 'simmering' crises may be lurking in your organization.

To do this, you need to establish both internal and external communications links that will alert you to the situation.

First, the people who work for you are almost always the first to know that there is a problem. The trick is to get them to alert you as soon as possible, without them feeling that they may be jeopardizing themselves. The 'stitch in time' adage remains as true as ever in crisis communications, and the earlier an issue is dealt with, the better. It is also important to let employees know that the problem has been tackled, because that will send the signal that you are a management that is confident enough to deal with difficult situations. Without that assurance they will think twice about notifying problems as they arise.

How can employees voice their concerns in the first place? Much will depend on the nature of the issue, so it is worth considering the following:

- **Staff newsletters or in-house magazines**. These are an obvious source of information about employee concerns but are often flawed by local conditions. Do the contributors feel free to express full and frank opinions about the company or organization? More often than not, in-house publications are referred to as *Pravda* after the communist party newspaper that was purely a mouthpiece for the Soviet authorities, so the answer may be 'no'. If people do feel unconstrained, are their comments read and taken seriously by the management who can put things right? Often, sadly, the answer is again 'no'.
- **Bulletin boards**. These days, they can be physical entities in public parts of the workplace or electronic on the internal e-mail system. Again, people may

be reluctant to air issues of concern. Notes can be posted anonymously on boards of both the physical or electronic variety but what if someone recognizes the handwriting or checks the server to reveal their identity?
- **Union or staff representatives**. These people often offer a good avenue for airing concerns and are a legitimate route, but only if the company or organization is unionized or has staff committees. Many organizations have neither. Even if they have, some issues may conflict with the interests of the union or committee, and the complaint or negative issue may get buried as a result.
- **Suggestion boxes**. Again, these are a useful and often anonymous way of airing a grievance, but they are open to abuse and observations are often ignored.
- **Appraisal systems**. Appraisals are by far the best approach to the problem generally although if the situation is urgent, they may not be appropriate. We often ask human resource directors whether their appraisal system allows for an employee to express concerns about the nature of their work or issues that could become a crisis. The answer is often that the issue has never even been thought about. Appraisals, they say, are for the manager to express an opinion on the performance of the individual and for the employee to respond. This is a little shortsighted in our view, given the valuable feedback that can come from an employee no matter how low or high in the organization.

Legislation in the form of the Public Interest Disclosure Act 1998 offers protection to people who are categorized as 'whistle-blowers'. The Act was introduced because a growing number of people found themselves vulnerable to dismissal or victimization as a direct result of them alerting management to an internal problem.

Quite often, the original issue would not be serious enough in itself to constitute a crisis. It would only become one when the frustrated whistle-blower decided to alert outside audiences, including the media, because not enough notice was being taken of their complaint.

A PROACTIVE APPROACH

All the situations we have mentioned in this chapter so far are characterized by management having to rely on their staff to alert them to potential problems. However, there is also a case for a more proactive approach. A crisis team does not have to wait for trouble to come to them. They can undertake the parallel role of 'risk auditing'.

This involves a regular, comprehensive, review of the activities of each department. Obviously, the cooperation of key members of that team is required, but most of the review body should be from other parts of the organization. Ideally, it should also include an independent person from outside who can bring a fresh eye to the subject.

To give the exercise teeth, the review team should report at regular intervals to the management committee or board of directors with their findings and recommendations about actions that are required. If serious 'simmering' issues have been uncovered, the crisis team can then get to work on neutralizing them before they become a full-blown emergency. A continuous risk review can utilize the skills of the crisis team without it ever having to meet in anger – prevention and cure rolled into one!

The principles underlying the internal machinery for issue identification and crisis-handling also apply to situations that might arise from external sources. Suppliers, customers and other stakeholders can be valuable to you by flagging up issues that they may be concerned about. However, if you are to remain in command of events, there must be a process which encourages them to liaise. Their risk assessment and crisis management procedures should complement your own.

The following steps could be taken by almost every company and organization. Every year at the meeting with your auditors and other accountants, make sure that there is an agenda item covering risk and crisis issues. It may be that these people have expressed a concern that, either by oversight or a misguided sense of discretion, has not been passed on. Outside consultants, like auditors, spend a great deal of time in their clients' offices and will often become privy to scandal and gossip. Since they are trained only to look for financial irregularities they may not pass their concerns on. They should be encouraged to do so.

Similarly, make sure that valued clients are regularly met. When the discussion is complete or the contract signed or renewed, why not ask: 'What are we doing right and what can we improve?' The resulting answers could be beneficial. It often strikes us as odd that companies put much effort into finding out why they have lost business but vary rarely bother to find out precisely why they have won a new contract or retained an existing one.

Losing business does not automatically mean that you have a crisis, but the underlying reasons for having done so might.

LEARNING POINTS

- ◆ Establish internal and external links to identify 'simmering' crises.
- ◆ Employees are often the first to know.

UNDERSTANDING CRISES AND THE THEORY OF COMMUNICATION

- ◆ A 'stitch in time' always works.
- ◆ Use all available means to get early warning.
- ◆ Appraisals can be valuable for finding out bad news.
- ◆ Always protect 'whistle-blowers'.
- ◆ Consider risk auditing.
- ◆ Set up appropriate procedures for hearing customers' and clients' concerns.

6 Science versus emotion

It may seem odd to have a bit of psychology within a book about crisis management, but it should be clear by now that, to be effective in handling a crisis or an emergency, you must have well-prepared and clear lines of internal and external communications.

That is only possible if you have people in key management positions who think seriously about communicating and are good at it themselves. They must recognize it as a skill and encourage others to acquire the necessary expertise. There are, however, stumbling blocks that must be identified and remedied.

Within every organization there are high percentages of people who have been trained in the so-called 'logical' disciplines such as science, engineering, accountancy and the law. Their subjects at school, college and university would have been based on logic of the A plus B equals C variety. While those studies helped them achieve the position they now hold, the more senior they have become, the more their logical minds have been encouraged.

Most senior management reports, for example, are logical in structure. They start with an outline of the situation (usually a problem), they survey various potential solutions and reach a number of conclusions. The whole thing is then rounded off with recommendations that usually involve the need to authorize financial or political support within the business. All very logical and precise.

Problems arise when you expect the self-same people to deliver the same information in oral form. Their natural response is to try to turn the written word into what we call 'speak speak'.

Why should this be a concern in a crisis? Simply because an emergency situation immediately puts pressure on the communications system and, since speed is of the essence, much of what might normally have been communicated by e-mail or memo has to be switched to word of mouth. If the person involved comes from a logical discipline and finds it difficult to communicate orally, their problem might exacerbate the crisis rather then help resolve it.

A further complicating factor is that a sudden or unexpected event is often technical in nature but has an impact on human beings who may not have been trained to think logically.

It is here that 'science' confronts 'emotion'.

Within any organization, people working in sales and marketing and human resources may well fall into the category of 'emotional thinkers'. Their jobs involve dealing with people at a human level, and they are usually skilled in observing how the human psyche works.

Many key external audiences fall into the same category. The media, community groups, environmentalists and some investors may all be driven by emotion, rather than logic. Not for them the clean conclusions of physics and chemistry but the fuzzy world of sociology, anthropology or art history. Their response to a communication that is heavily technical or logical may be to switch off or become angry. The following example from the railways demonstrates this point.

EXAMPLE 6.1
Train at Victoria Station

A few years ago, one of the old British Rail-era slam door trains, fairly full with passengers, arrived at Victoria faster then usual because there was a problem with the brakes. The driver was unable to stop the train, and it hit the buffers at considerable speed. The second carriage reared up on the first causing quite a bit of damage and about a dozen passengers were slightly injured and needed to be taken to hospital.

Someone on the platform filmed the aftermath of the incident with a video camera and this made dramatic coverage on the South East TV news that evening. There were pictures of the twisted train and stretchers being lifted into ambulances and a script describing what had happened.

In regional news terms it was a big story – not so much because of the crash itself, since there were mercifully few injuries, but because of the disruption to train services. There were pictures of blank departure boards and half a dozen travellers were asked about their delays. These were considerable since the news was being transmitted right in the middle of the rush hour.

The presenter in the studio linked from a video report on the incident live to the station where the reporter began a live update about the transport chaos that, he said, would last for many hours. He then turned to a man beside him who turned out to be the managing director of the train company involved and put a question to the effect of 'what happened?'.

> The MD, an engineer by training, immediately launched into an answer that told the viewers how delighted he was that the train (that was more than 25 years old) had not broken up on impact! He said that his people were amazed at the resilience of the train. Not a word about the injured people, the cancelled trains and the disgruntled commuters!
>
> One can only have sympathy for him; the engineer in him forced him to think logically and subsume his human instincts. When he got home that night he probably told his wife how awful it had been and how sorry he was for the injured and those who had been delayed in their travel.
>
> It is a pity, however, that he did not express those thoughts on television in front of millions of viewers instead of putting a positive engineering gloss on the incident.
>
> In truth, on the night of an accident like this there is very little upside for the company involved. The best that can be done is to put your emotional instincts first, apologize for the inconvenience, send sympathy to the injured and their families, and pledge complete cooperation in the inquiry that will surely follow. Above all, you must come over as an individual human being who has been touched.

If we accept, then, that in a crisis much more of the communications will be oral, it is worth highlighting what this means in practical terms. All verbal communications consist of the following elements:

- the messages – preferably no more than three key items
- the audience – the people the messages are aimed at
- the medium – the method of delivering the messages to the audience.

Of the above three elements it often surprises people to learn that one is vastly more important than the other two put together – it is the audience every time.

When you look at the issue logically, it really does not matter how good the messages are or how good the medium of delivery is, if you have misread the audience then there has been no effective communication. In a crisis, speedy communications to many audiences simultaneously is especially crucial.

In Chapter 5 we emphasized the need to identify key internal and external audiences. However, it is equally important to select the sort of messages that they will want to hear in an emergency. If there is no overlap between what you want to say and what they want to hear then there will have been no communication. Misunderstandings, inaccuracies, rumour and mayhem will ensue.

Let us take the obvious example of the managing director of a medium-sized company who has to announce 250 redundancies. He has to give the news to some of the affected staff in the works canteen. Later in the day, he has to brief investors about the same situation.

It is more than likely that his message to the workforce will be different in tone to that which he delivers to his investors. To one audience the news is bad and personal, and they are likely to be angry. To the other, the news may be encouraging because the measures proposed cut overheads and may put the company back into profit.

In a crisis, decisions have to be taken quickly about what key audiences should hear which key messages. This is often referred to as 'spin-doctoring' – in our view a perfectly legitimate practice but one that has fallen into disrepute because of its association in the world of politics with lies, distortions and duplicity. What it actually means is to take the same set of facts and emphasize the positive, rather than the negative, aspects in respect of differing audiences.

News is often like electricity; there are always positives for every negative if you give yourself time to think it all through and tease them out.

In crisis training we always encourage executives who may find their production methods or procedures questioned in the event of an accident to think through why they do things the way they do.

If you do this carefully enough in advance you are much more likely to be able to respond confidently when someone asks, 'Wasn't this an accident waiting to happen?'

Of course, selecting messages for key audiences is only part of the problem. You must also consider the way in which the information is to be delivered. Research has indicated that 60 per cent of the effectiveness of business communications is attributable to non-verbal elements. It is, in effect, not what you say, but how you say it that counts.

Meaning is communicated by pace, pitch, tone, timing, subtext and unconscious discourse. All of which adds up to the fact that, in a crisis, all your messages must be clear, honest and delivered in a fashion that forces the audience to believe you.

The average intelligent human being can absorb 15 words per second if they read information but only three words per second if someone delivers the same information orally. This means that every word must count – particularly when you and your audience are under pressure.

When we exhort managers to use simple language and drop the jargon we often ask them to complete the 'fresh fish test' (see example 6.1). Years later they will say: 'I remember you. You're the bloke who does the fresh fish test!'

> **EXAMPLE 6.2**
> **The Fresh Fish Test**
> Consider the following message:
> FRESH
> FISH
> SOLD
> HERE
> DAILY
>
> Remove an unessential word. Then another, then another, then another until you are left with just one word: 'FISH'. That is all that is necessary.

If you have more than 25 words on a visual aid, the audience will not absorb it all – no matter how long it is put up in front of them.

> **EXAMPLE 6.3**
> **Rule of Five**
> TRY TO MAKE SURE THAT
> THERE ARE NO MORE THAN
> FIVE WORDS TO THE LINE
> OR FIVE LINES DOWN IN
> ANY VISUAL MATERIAL YOU PRESENT

Try subjecting your key messages to what we call the 'Rule of Five': no more than five clear words across an index card, which acts as a prompt, and no more than five lines long. Subjecting what you have to say to this test makes an announcement or interview clear and concise with a minimum of jargon or 'management-speak'. This is important because, in a crisis, a speaker's credibility can be destroyed if the audiences believe that the truth is being obscured by complicated language.

One of the many tasks for the communications specialist and spokesperson on a crisis team is to make sure that all messages are simple, clear and consistent. No matter how complicated the issue, it has been conclusively proven that an audience will only receive and understand three key elements. So, why clutter up your communications with more?

The challenge is, of course, to make sure that they are three key things that a particular audience is interested in hearing.

It is also a good idea to illustrate each of your messages with a very specific example of what you are talking about. The audience will remember the example long after they have forgotten the detail of the message. This is very effective when giving media interviews.

Let us imagine that there has been a fire in a sports clothing factory. After expressing regret for what has happened and thanking the fire brigade for their valiant efforts the spokesperson says:

> It is a sad day for all of us. We employ 250 people here and supply clothing to millions of sports fans. [*key messages: sadness, employment and customers needs*].
>
> Our employees will be worrying about their jobs but, most importantly, fans will be worried that they may not be able to buy their shirts for next season. We are already talking to the clubs to make sure that there will be no disruption to supply. [*an example affecting people*].

A clear statement of this sort addresses the emotion behind the issue. It expresses in plain language that you are in control and implies, without saying so, that everything will be all right.

These are all-important messages for internal and external audiences: staff, customers and other interested parties such as banks, investors and suppliers.

LEARNING POINTS

- ◆ 'Logical' thinkers are not necessarily the best communicators.
- ◆ A crisis demands clear communications.
- ◆ The challenge is to try to get 'science' attitudes closer to 'emotional' ones.
- ◆ What the audience wants to hear is as important as what you want to say.
- ◆ Try to analyse what you do and how you do it and then sort how best to explain it in non-technical terms.
- ◆ Sixty per cent of the effectiveness of communications is attributable to non-verbal language.
- ◆ In a crisis, your messages must be clear, honest and believable.
- ◆ Do not use jargon.

7 How the media works

In any crisis, the most important of all the key external audiences are the media – print publications of all types, the broadcasting outlets and, now, the new technologies involved in the World Wide Web. Planning how the media should be dealt with in a crisis is the task of the communications member of the crisis team. Handling the situation can only be done effectively if you have a clear idea of how each branch of the media family works. (See Appendix 4, Media Handling, in Part III.) Each of them disseminates information (good and bad, accurate and inaccurate) so fast and to so many audiences that you need procedures in place in order to control the information they receive from you. Just as importantly, you also need parallel systems to find out what information they are getting from other sources.

Every journalist knows that the faster you get on to and ahead of a story or an issue the better. If your business or organization is in the centre of a newsworthy incident or event you need to have a similar mental attitude and the ability to act swiftly and decisively. Efficient media handling requires specialist skills and a detailed knowledge of what is required.

JOURNALISTS IN GENERAL

Journalists tend to be individualists who, by the very nature of their job, act as a pack. They have an instinct that makes them dangerous to those with something to hide or a miracle for organizations that want to promote something. How often have 'star' performers (whether in showbusiness or commercial business) been created by the media only to be destroyed by them later? The few that survive to see out a 'complete' career are usually those who have actively courted journalists and accepted the rough with the smooth in terms of coverage.

Who are these people who choose to make their living as journalists? Notwithstanding the proliferation of media studies courses at colleges and universities they are still drawn from a vast pool of other sources. They are often specialist practitioners in a given profession who are attracted by what they see as the glamorous life. Sometimes they have been forced out of their previous career and turn to journalism in order to pay the bills (ex-politicians come to mind). All too often nowadays, they are successful individuals who turn themselves into 'star' reporters or columnists almost as an extension of their 'day jobs' (as sports personalities and actors, for example). Because journalists are such individualists it is hard to generalize about them but, in our experience, the key to their success or otherwise lies in their ability or otherwise to maintain an interest in a subject long enough to be able to tell a story about it to others.

Long before literacy became almost universal, people and societies communicated events to each other by storytelling, and journalism is an extension of that art. Stories have a beginning, a middle and an end, and a news story follows a specific formula.

The opening of a news item is known as the 'lead' and usually comprises two or three paragraphs that sum up the whole story. The rest of it is then written in descending order of importance until, towards the end, the minor quotations or statistics are given. Depending on your level of interest in the piece, your eyes gradually go down until the end is reached, or you get bored and move on to something else. From a technical point of view this format is much easier to edit; the sub-editor simply cuts from the bottom of the story if space is short.

Much the same applies in broadcasting, except that the viewer or listener doesn't have the luxury of leaving the story unless they switch off.

Why do you need to know all this when planning for a crisis? Simply because if you know how journalists do their business and craft their finished product, the easier it will be to control the information you make available. As a result, your agenda stands a better chance of being reported accurately.

It is often forgotten that the journalists have another key audience for their work, quite apart from the readers, listeners or viewers. Important as these groups may be, they do not generally dictate who is employed or not on a publication or media broadcast. That power usually resides with the editor or the publisher who usually base their judgements on whether or not their employees are successful. And the criteria for success? It can be summed up quite simply as: 'Have they beaten the competition?' So, to journalists, key audiences are: editors, other journalists and, coming a distant third, the people who buy what they produce.

During crisis management courses on dealing with the media we often ask the participants if they believe that journalists wake up in the morning asking themselves, 'How can I distort the truth today?' Those who have been bruised by the media in the past often nod their heads in the affirmative but, when phrased like that, the notion is pretty ludicrous. Of course, there are exceptions to the rule but, generally speaking, journalists try to get things right. How often they fail and why goes to the heart of the breakdown of trust between organizations and journalists, particularly in a crisis.

One reason for inaccuracy and misrepresentation is often unappreciated by those outside the news and current affairs business – namely, the pressure to complete stories by tight deadlines. Journalists work long hours, often at breakneck speed, to beat the competition at the lowest possible cost.

Nowadays publishers and broadcasting stations are run by accountants who have little or no understanding about what journalism is all about. It is not their fault; it just happens to be a slice of life that they have not been trained to understand. In daily journalism they see journalists idling about for much of the working day with apparently little to occupy them. Yet, long after the accountants have been tucked up in bed, those same journalists are in manic activity to finish the story and beat the competition up against those magic words: the deadline.

THE DEADLINE

Put simply, the deadline is the hour of the day or night when the journalists say goodbye to their attempts to make sense of a story and submit it for publication.

If a crucial part of your story is missing because you have failed to provide information in time for the journalist's deadline, two things are lost. First, you have squandered the opportunity to put your side of the story on record and, second, the publication or broadcaster will no longer trust you as a provider of information.

Always establish as early as possible with each journalist when they require information, statements, pictures or facilities. If you cannot meet the deadline for any reason tell them as soon as possible.

Not long ago, the head of corporate affairs of a major television production company died suddenly. He was little known outside the world of public relations, but his obituaries universally praised him as a man and for his skills. Specifically, each one mentioned that, no matter how much pressure he was under or how damaging the event may be to his employer, *he always returned calls and met deadlines.*

Given the pack instincts of most journalists, one can only imagine the opprobrium reserved for the representatives of organizations who do not do the same.

The trick, then, in a crisis, is to make the journalist's task as simple as possible. To help in this it is worth remembering that most of them are born with characteristics that are denied to most people. First, a propensity towards idleness. Despite deadlines, competitors and long tense hours at work, they will always take the easy option if it is offered.

Second, bullshit detectors. If you appear to be slow-moving in meeting their desires, they immediately take this as a sign of evasiveness or a desire to mislead even when nothing could be further from the truth. A snappy response with good information to meet their deadlines will guarantee that they will love you forever. Well, to be more accurate, they will love you until the next time something negative happens to your organization.

We tell you exactly how to package up relevant information in Appendix 2, 'The Spokesperson', but if you follow strict guidelines your ability to sound confident, open and friendly will be enhanced.

During a crisis, when both you and the journalists are under pressure, a lack of friendliness, openness and confidence on your part may cause them to go elsewhere for their information – and that will be a source that is not under your control. Control over the situation is key to handing the media and, whether you appreciate this or not, you do have significant elements of control in the face of journalistic enquiries: control over when, how and with what detail you are prepared to deal with them; control over the exact information you are prepared to reveal; and control over whether they can go back to their editor and say that they have a balanced and well-sourced story.

Just consider for a moment the pressure on a reporter who has not been able to substantiate their story with information from you. Their editors will be less than impressed and may amend the article to reflect the lack of comment from you. Remember, too, that 'no comment' actually means 'guilty as charged' in the eyes of journalists and their audiences.

There are sophisticated checks and balances within news organizations to establish whether a reporter has produced a true and accurate reflection of an interview or briefing.

If we are called in to conduct an inquest into why a company suffered financial damage as a result of news coverage the first thing we do is ask for the dossier covering the journalists' enquiries and how they were dealt with. What interviews were given? What records taken? It is truly amazing how often we are told that no such record exists: 'It was all done on the phone.'

There are certain routines that must be followed if a crisis strikes or if you suspect that negative material is going to be reported against you. No matter who takes the initial enquiry, usually by phone, they should find out and write down exactly who the journalist is and who they are reporting for. In addition, they should find out their deadline and what information they want from you.

Information, statistics, interviews, pictures, videos or an opportunity to come and see you or your operations?

Ideally, this initial chat should also include the following questions:

- What information have you got already?
- Who else are you talking to?
- Have you completed those interviews already?
- What is the angle of your story at the moment?

In effect, you are interviewing the journalists about themselves without volunteering any information yourself.

When you feel that you have found out as much as possible, concoct any excuse to terminate the discussion and promise to get back to them later. That gives you breathing space to analyse the situation and consult with others about whether you want to contribute to the article or participate in the broadcast. If you suspect that the item may be negative, ask them to fax or e-mail their request. This will form the first part of a paper trail that must now be kept until the matter is resolved and you have full control over the situation.

How, then, do the individual branches of the news media work? There is a saying 'a lie is halfway around the world before the truth can get its boots on' and in today's high-speed IT-driven world, that has never been more true. Fibre optics and satellites instantly transmit not only the written word, but also still and moving pictures, so it is important, in a crisis, to monitor any coverage and, if necessary, inject your own messages on to those high-speed media operations.

NEWS AGENCIES

In every town almost all over the world there will be at least one agency that specializes in news. They are the unsung heroes of the news business because they keep an ear on everything from the local courts and councils to the emergency services and utilities. They make judgements about what is news and then sell it up the line to the national news agency. Every country has one of these, and some have become world famous – for example, Reuters, originally headquartered in London but now an international operation, Agence France-Presse in France and Associated Press in the United States, Tass in Russia.

In Britain the domestic national news agency is called The Press Association and it acts as a key tip-off service for all the news editors of publications and broadcasting organizations in the UK. Otherwise known as a 'wire service' after the now-defunct tickertapes, they provide a constant stream of news about events, occasionally pulling together the main points and sending them out as 'leads'. These are the seed corn of the news business because they alert editors about what is happening, so that staff reporters and correspondents can be assigned to, or confirm, events and issues.

The Press Association, or PA as it is known, will almost certainly be one of the first news agencies to hear about your crisis. If it is a sudden piece of news it will be given a priority rating to alert the newsrooms.

- A **Snap** is an important story but of no world-shattering importance: for example, 'It is being reported that XYZ Fashions, one of the largest makers of women's bras in the UK is being taken over by ABC, the American-owned and world's biggest manufacturer of female underwear.'

  Almost every news editor in the country will go for that story because, in addition to being a moderately interesting business item, it also offers a wholesome excuse to feature pictures of scantily clad models.
- The next order of priority is a **bulletin**, usually a one-line piece of information of major importance: for example, 'Explosion in main shopping centre in Manchester. Injuries reported. Cause unknown.'

  That would result in the mobilization of almost every major news-gathering organization in the country since, until told otherwise, they will expect it to have been a terrorist bomb. If it turns out to have been a gas leak then things will be scaled down rapidly.
- The absolute highest priority is a **flash**: for example, 'Pope dead.'

  This signals a world-shattering event that will be reported everywhere and affect millions of people.

If you are connected with the publicly quoted XYZ bra company and this confirms a deal that you have been working on for a long time, the news agency item quoted above constitutes a crisis. Its wording ('it is being reported that') signals that it has not come from a formal announcement made by either you or the American company. This means that there has been a leak of information and things are out of your own control. You need to regain control as soon as possible, but there may be an inherent problem. If the news breaks during the stock market trading day there may be difficulties in saying too much since it will be price-sensitive information. It is under these circumstances that instant legal/investment and public relations advice must be sought and acted upon.

If you are a high-street retailer with outlets in Manchester, the bulletin item concerning the explosion should immediately signal a calling together of your crisis team. Whether terrorism is involved or not, you will probably be called on to move quickly on personnel issues, public relations and all the external audience items that have been identified under the 'sudden' disaster part of the plan.

The flash event featuring the pope is not, in itself, a direct crisis for anyone outside the College of Cardinals that has to select another one. But it could constitute a crisis for any company or organization dealing with Italy. Transport, tourism and all day-to-day business will be disrupted by the death of the pontiff, and contingency plans will have to be implemented immediately.

The important thing to remember about the news agencies or 'wire services' is that they are as accessible to you as anyone else. If you have a statement, comment or correction, give it to them first. This way, all the other news organizations will see it simultaneously. It only takes a fax, telephone call or an e-mail, although you must always make it easy for them to come back to you to confirm that you are who you say you are.

Also remember the communications links used by the emergency services are prime sources of information for news agencies. If your crisis involves them in any way, the agency journalists will hear about it immediately. Make it part of your crisis communications planning to expect journalists to turn up at the same time, or even earlier, than the emergency services.

THE TRADE AND BUSINESS PRESS

There is an assumption that, because a journalist works for a publication that specializes in your sector, they are not only experts on your business but can also be expected to deal with you sympathetically. Both may be true, but do not bank on it.

Writers for a trade magazine may well have a great deal of general expertise but cannot know as much as you about the subject. It is also worth remembering that first and foremost, they are journalists and will therefore want to find exclusive stories that beat their competition.

News reporters often use the trade press as a primary source, particularly during an emergency event when they need to report at speed. There is no quicker way to glean expert knowledge than by a chat with a specialist writer who knows about the business concerned. The same specialist writers are also good sources for the analysts who work for the investment banks and finance houses. To some extent they feed off each other, so keep your messages to both as clear and consistent as possible.

Our advice is to maintain close relations with trade publication editors and journalists in bad times as well as good. They hate companies which only want to talk to them when they have 'good' news. While cultivating this open approach, however, exercise caution at all times. As with all dealings with journalists, make sure that you know in advance as much as possible about what they know and what they want from you. Establish what their deadlines are and get back to them as fast as possible with the information that you want to see in print.

This should be in the form of approximately three key points illustrated by examples of what you mean. The trade press will be more inclined to put in technical information and statistics, but do not overload them. It is crucial to establish that they really know what they are talking about because trade press journalists, in particular, have a habit of giving the impression that they know more than they actually do. If, having given the information or interview, you have any doubts, follow up with a fax or e-mail outlining your key points and the raw information that you will be happy to see in print.

We are often asked whether you can request, or indeed demand, to see articles before they are printed. The usual answer is 'no' because journalists carefully guard their right to put an item together on their own terms. Trade press articles are, however, sometimes submitted for you to look at in advance, so that any factual errors can be corrected. Trade press writers do not want to look foolish to their competitors. In an ideal world, if you have done your job in finding out exactly what they are writing about and have responded accordingly, there should be no need to ask to see it in advance.

A word about individual journalists on trade publications. We find that some of them 'take against' certain companies or organizations for a variety of reasons. By all means try to get such 'hostile' elements on your side but, if they become a persistent problem, drop all contact and, if necessary, let their editor know the reason why.

There is absolutely no reason why you should cooperate with an individual who regularly writes negative or inaccurate things about you. Some companies are reluctant to complain, but this is a mistake for several reasons. First, you are entitled to have a balanced and fair report; second, damaging statements should be corrected; and, third, editors do not like employing journalists who attract too many complaints. Even more important, you need to establish corrections in the publication's database of information about you. If you fail to do this, the wrong material will be repeated time and again.

Often, a trade journalist will contact your company or organization to say that they are writing an article about X for Y publication. During your preparations make sure that they are telling the truth about both the subject-matter and the publication as many freelance journalists get hold of a piece of negative information and blow it out of all proportion in order to sell it to publication Y. Of course, not all freelance writers are trouble, and many trade magazines assign special projects to freelances, but it is important to find out exactly what their status is.

NEWSPAPERS

THE NATIONALS

Although the distinctions can often be blurred, there are broadly three categories of national newspaper: 'quality broadsheets', 'mid-market tabloids' and 'downmarket tabloids' otherwise known as the 'red tops' because of their distinctive name-plate mastheads.

Quality broadsheets

The quality press in Britain includes *The Financial Times*, *The Times* and the *Daily Telegraph*, along with the *Guardian* and the *Independent*. They all operate on a similar basis, although their production methods and design vary. However their main difference lies in their political stance as reflected in their opinion pages and, often, in the tone of their news coverage.

At one time, not so long ago, it was broadly true that *The Financial Times*, *The Times* and the *Daily Telegraph* were all solid backers of the Conservative Party whereas the *Independent* leant towards the Liberal Democrats and the *Guardian* supported the Labour Party. However, with the emergence of New Labour and the decline of the Conservative Party, the political sands have shifted and those lines of support have twisted and changed.

Although the quality broadsheets have a relatively low readership compared to that of the tabloid media, their influence on public life can be considerable because their readers tend to be influential in business, politics and the professions.

National broadsheet journalists have reached the top of their profession, and they have not got there by being easily soft-soaped. They are also in vicious competition with each other and are tenacious in their search for information about you from any source they can muster. They work very fast and are often better at finding out details about your organization than you are.

We always recommend that whoever is in charge of communications in a crisis gets to know personally at least one member of staff at each of the quality broadsheet national newspapers. A good use of those contacts can make the difference between receiving totally negative coverage when things go wrong and receiving neutral or even positive coverage.

Mid-market tabloids

This sector takes in the *Daily Mail* and the *Daily Express* mass-circulation tabloids which carry quite a bit of clout thanks to their appeal to 'middle England'

and, particularly, consumers. Millions of households read them every day, and a negative story or some campaigning journalism can be very damaging.

Politicians and other policy-makers are very wary of upsetting these newspapers, because their owners carry powerful mandates through the circulation figures, and their editors are of high calibre with an uncanny capacity for spotting shifts in public opinion. They encourage a dialogue with their readers and, when they identify an issue, they pursue it ruthlessly knowing that it will sell newspapers. They are particularly keen on consumer and environmental issues, animal rights, medicine, fitness, personal finance and property – everything, in fact, that has an impact on the so-called 'ordinary' household.

If you or your organization gets in the way of a tabloid story, or indeed if you trigger one, then watch out. Your crisis planning should build in the ability to be tipped off that a major tabloid newspaper is pursuing you. This can be difficult, however; the tabloids operate in complete secrecy and only reveal their story at the very last minute, just before they plan to print it. If it is a major exclusive, they even hold it back from their first edition so that their rivals can't find out about it.

If you find yourself in this position there is often nothing that can be done immediately, although there is one avenue that you can exploit if you act swiftly enough. Most tabloid stories are based on a nugget of truth, but they also contain substantial amounts of inaccuracies and distortions. So, when the publication reveals its information, make careful notes, particularly about the things that are wrong. A swift consultation within your organization should produce a speedy rebuttal that must be faxed or e-mailed immediately to the publication's news editor. Both methods of delivery make them timed documents and are useful evidence in any subsequent complaint about the publication's behaviour.

On the night shift of any newspaper is a trained lawyer who sits with the news editor and staff to advise on the wisdom of running a story that might result in legal action. Once you have signalled your unhappiness about some of the facts in advance of publication, the news editor might just hold off until the story can be properly 'stood up', to use the journalistic jargon.

The key, as always, is to take action fast. You cannot go into committee to decide what action to take but must delegate to two or three people within the management team who are authorized to move with speed.

The 'red tops'

This is the generic name for the *Daily Mirror*, the *Sun*, the *Daily Star* and others because of their distinctive mastheads. These 'downmarket tabloids' may be derided on account of their sensationalist approach and almost obsessive sexual content but, over the years, they have proved to be dangerously potent opinion-formers.

'It was the *Sun* wot won it' was a headline after a general election, and the political pundits agreed that this was, indeed, the truth. The *Sun* can shift voter sentiment, and the politicians know it. Tony Blair, just before be became prime minister, famously flew halfway around the world to Australia for a meeting with the publisher Rupert Murdoch to get his editorial support. One reason why Mr Blair knew all about the power of the tabloid press was because his close personal friend and head of communications, Alistair Campbell, had been a senior political journalist on the *Daily Mirror*.

Another tabloid obsession is the Royal Family (or the 'Firm' as they are reported to call themselves). They have been tested in crisis management communications over the years – not only tested but shown to be woefully unable to understand the first principles. In fact, most negative tabloid reporting about their activities has been absolutely accurate, despite their denials at the time. Consider past stories about Princess Margaret and Peter Townsend, Princess Margaret and Anthony Armstrong Jones, Princess Margaret and Roddy Lewellyn, Princess Anne to marry and then divorce, a whole raft of stories about Prince Charles and the Princess of Wales, all initially rubbished as tabloid mischief but subsequently confirmed as being true.

The Royal Family has made several attempts to get professional communications advice, with mixed success. Mixed, because the Palace has robbed itself of the one quality that is needed in crisis communications work – credibility. That has disappeared because individual members of the Royal Family have found it hard to tell the truth even to their closest communications advisers. As a result, tabloid editors have made even more determined efforts to dish the dirt. It is a spiral of mistrust that only the principals can put right.

Arguably, the real issue has not been each individual story, but a growing public frustration with the Royal Family which has been picked up by the tabloid editors. A monarchy is good, goes the message, but the family itself, in the eyes of most of the public, has became too big. A crisis management expert would advise the Queen, the Duke of Edinburgh and Prince Charles to keep up the good work with as much publicity as they like, but encourage the others to do as little as possible for as long as possible.

THE REGIONAL DAILY PRESS

In our opinion the regional daily press comprises the most powerful publications in the land and should be treated accordingly. Not only are they read by millions of people every day, but they are written by local journalists about events and places familiar to readers. This gives them a credibility that cannot be matched by their national newspaper counterparts.

It may well be that your crisis will find the regional press first and, if so, you can expect the news agencies and the national newspapers to be not far behind.

It is a good idea to foster warm professional relationships with regional journalists and make sure what they report about you is accurate. It is always worth remembering that, within every regional newspaper, there are a handful of ambitious journalists who want to break into the national publications. To do that they will pursue crisis stories and investigate them. Try to find out who they are and treat them with exceptional care.

LOCAL NEWSPAPERS

It is a broad generality, but the more local a publication is to your operations the more favourable it tends to be in its coverage. This will be particularly true if you employ a significant number of local people and advertise with the newspaper.

None of this will be much help in a crisis, however.

Again, the most sound advice is to build a relationship with the editors and reporters that endures whether the news is good or bad. If they respect you for past actions, it will have an impact on the tone of their reporting. This is particularly important since they may well be a key source of information for regional and national reporters when they are trying to find out more about you. If the local newspaper editor describes you as a good, helpful and open company or organization, that opinion will carry weight.

BROADCASTING

RADIO

Since the 1960s there has been an explosion in the number of BBC and commercial local radio stations in the UK. Before then, the only 'wireless' was that provided on national networks by the BBC. This all changed with the advent of pirate radio stations broadcasting from fixed platforms or ships anchored in international waters (such as Radio Caroline). There were also stations based in Europe that beamed programmes into the UK, such as Radio Luxembourg.

Even 'Auntie Beeb' could read the signs and began to widen its appeal by broadcasting rock and pop music. It also established half a dozen local radio stations as an experiment. After a slow beginning, they began to get an increasingly favourable reaction and, when the government eventually relaxed the broadcasting regulations, commercial stations also began to spring up all over the country.

Today there are hundreds of stations, all of whom are constantly hungry for news material. This makes them attractive outlets for positive news, but they can spring into life in a more negative way should crisis hit you.

The important thing to remember about radio is that it is an intimate medium that comes into people's homes, workplaces and cars. Listeners are almost always doing something else but, if you can immediately capture their attention, they can often be supportive.

The key, as usual, is to have two or three clear messages backed up by examples and delivered by a spokesperson with a powerful voice that can immediately cut through to the listener.

A pre-recorded interview may be done by a reporter who visits you with a small portable tape recorder. They will ask questions for about four or five minutes and then edit the material to something over two minutes, taking out the 'ums' and 'ers' in the process.

Try to get all your main points into the first answer and keep returning to them almost no matter what line of questioning comes up. Remember, it should be your agenda and not the reporter's – particularly in a time of crisis when you may be feeling on the defensive.

Another trick is to acknowledge the question without actually answering it. This is a favourite ploy of politicians, although most of them do it so badly that it gets noticed by listeners who become furious as a result. An interviewee who does it well is not rumbled.

Radio reporters are particularly partial to asking for an interview on the telephone at the drop of a hat. In such an event, try to avoid being bounced into doing something you are unprepared for and remember the golden rules: find out exactly what the interview is about, who else are they interviewing and take time to prepare your key messages and illustrations in advance. The radio station personnel will usually give you a special telephone number for the recording, but only use it when you are good and ready. It is also a useful tip to say to yourself beforehand 'This telephone is now becoming a microphone', because it is easy to find yourself becoming too relaxed with such a familiar instrument and saying something indiscreet.

Alternatively, the radio station may want you to participate in a 'phone-in' programme. Always check out this possibility in advance because many an interviewee has found themselves doing a live broadcast that suddenly becomes a listener discussion 'out of the blue'.

The formidable Margaret Thatcher once confessed that one of the few occasions when she felt totally out of control was during a televised phone-in, conducted as part of the *Nationwide* news programme, during an election campaign. A viewer from Bristol took her apart about the sinking of the Argentine warship, the *Belgrano*, during the Falklands War. The untrained housewife had prepared her material, but the prime minister had not and was made to look foolish.

One problem with phone-in programmes is that they often attract difficult people who are irrational or actually mad. Let them have their say, then take their name and say, for the benefit of the other listeners, 'I am quite happy to tackle that but, to let others have a chance on the air, perhaps I can call you back after the programme has finished.' This tactic may not always work, but it does demonstrate that you have the wider interests of the audience in mind and that you have sufficiently good judgement to isolate the one who is troublesome.

If you are given the option to go live on radio or recorded, try to go live – particularly if you have done some interviews before and feel comfortable with them. The reason for this is that radio tape is cheap, and an interviewer is more likely to be hostile in the knowledge that any overt hostility can be edited out later. In a live broadcast they have to keep the show going, they are being distracted by technical instructions and are consequently less likely to be aggressive.

In crisis planning it is a good idea to build in procedures for using local radio to make a public service announcement. This is not exactly a news and current affairs item, but circumstances may require it if there is any question of public danger or concern, as with fires, accidents or product recalls.

If you give an interview as an incident is unfolding always make sure that you give another one after it is all over. Public service announcements made during a crisis have a nasty habit of turning up as news items later.

TELEVISION

This is without doubt the most powerful news and current affairs medium that we have, but it is also the most transitory. While newspapers and magazines can hang around for ages and be read by scores of people over time (think of the dentist's waiting room), television is gone in an instant.

A crisis is usually meat and drink to television, particularly if it falls into the sudden disaster category. Drama usually means pictures, and television loves pictures.

Since most interviews on television last for less than two minutes and are sometimes edited down to a few seconds, everything that is said has to count.

Unlike radio, where people judge you by your voice, reactions to the visual medium are more complicated. It is estimated that people judge an interview mainly on how you look, your tone of voice and your clothes. Only a small percentage is based on what you are actually saying. As a result, great care must be taken to avoid anything that can be distracting, such as ties that are not properly knotted, unconventional suit designs or a delegate badge which the viewer will spend half the interview trying to read rather than paying attention to what you are saying.

With this in mind, it is hopeless to wait until the interview starts before deciding what you are going to say. Everything must be thought through in advance and each key message illustrated with an example. When the lights, camera and microphones start operating your brain has quite enough to do without thinking about what your message is. This is particularly relevant in a crisis because the metaphorical heat will be on, and the interviewer is likely to want to put you under pressure.

Do not submit.

Act as if you have knowledge to share rather than defending a position and under no circumstances lose your temper.

We find 'softening' phrases useful: for example, 'there is a lot of misunderstanding about this' or 'let's try to clear up some of the misunderstandings here'. It is also a good idea to use inclusive language because it is all too easy to use words that can suggest that the broadcast audience is 'out there' or in some way removed. It is worth getting into the habit of using the words 'we all' and 'everyone' in interviews.

We are often asked whether interviews are best done on location, in an office or a studio.

In our opinion, studios are intimidating places where you are in danger of being seen as just another 'talking head'. Doing the interview on your own territory is usually best, as long as you are setting the agenda. Make sure that you know exactly what the backdrop is and make yourself look comfortable. Also, try to limit the time you are available for the interview because, as in radio, videotape is cheap and, in a prerecorded session, it is easy for the interviewer to repeatedly ask the same question until they get the answer they are looking for and then edit out the repetitions to cover up the fact that the interviewee has been 'bullied' into the answer. Ten to fifteen minutes maximum is our recommendation, although it can easily be less if you are well-prepared and concise.

Always ask what the first question is going to be because it is in the programme-makers' interests to get the interview off to a strong start. Just one word of warning: there may be a delay or a distraction and the first question may suddenly change, so don't rely on it!

Most important, in a prerecorded radio or television interview, *the first question is not broadcast* so, in reality, you have total freedom to say exactly what you want in your first answer.

Should you appear live or recorded?

UNDERSTANDING CRISES AND THE THEORY OF COMMUNICATION

Again, if you feel comfortable with the medium, go live since it cannot be edited. Remember, though, that precisely the same applies if you make a mistake!

Should you do an interview in your office, never be seen sitting behind a desk as this creates a barrier between you and your audience. It is far better to arrange a couple of seats by a pot plant, a lamp, a bookcase or even a computer screen as long as the screen contents are not distracting. These are all softening features and make you look more natural.

A word about a form of interview that is becoming more popular with broadcasters because it is cheap (no expensive crews involved) and makes the best use of highly paid presenters – namely, the 'down the line' or 'remote' interview in which you are asked to go to a small studio, put in an earpiece, look into an automated camera and answer questions. You must have seen the sort of thing on the BBC's *Newsnight* programme where some frightened looking body looms up from Leeds or Manchester only to be told by Jeremy Paxman sitting in the London studio: 'You are in something of a bugger's muddle here aren't you?'

With this format, all the normal rules apply, but make sure that you look as relaxed as possible and try not to stare absolutely into the centre of the lens. Look at the little red light or the maker's name on the top of the camera in order to minimize the chances of you looking like a rabbit caught in the headlights of a car.

NEW TECHNOLOGIES

All the types of media we have mentioned up to now can be classed as 'conventional' in the sense that they have been around for some time and almost everyone in the land is familiar with the general way in which they work. The media creates what is known as a 'news cycle' that makes it necessary to update all information on a situation at regular intervals of the press or broadcasting day. Morning, lunchtime and evening bulletins reflect this convention. Nowadays, however, new technologies in the media are tending to erode that 'news cycle' by constantly demanding updated information as it becomes available: for example, 24-hour satellite television and cable news stations want a continuous flow of news.

Your crisis communications plan has to accommodate this new development, and your spokespeople no longer have the luxury of knowing that they may have up to six hours before the next briefing. It rather depends on your degree of control over the raw material. If other parties are involved, it is almost impossible to avoid continuous updates.

This not the place to go into matters 'digital', but your crisis plan has to acknowledge that the mass media is now moving into an era where television, information technology and telecommunications can all 'talk to each other'. It is now perfectly possible to sit on a South Sea island beach and listen to the *Today* programme through your laptop computer. Furthermore, you can interact with the programme by e-mail.

Information is communicated faster than ever and your corporate crisis plan has to reflect that fact. As part of your media monitoring you should keep a special eye on what is happening on your company website if you have one. Keep it up-to-date with all the information you are giving to the rest of the media and correct any misleading, untrue or distorted messages put on it by people who are hostile to you. There are what are collectively called 'suck sites' that are set up specifically to attack corporations and organizations. You must be seen to be in dialogue with them and correct inaccurate information immediately.

INVESTIGATIVE PROGRAMMES

In recent years investigative programmes have emerged in a number of guises – sometimes as consumer champions, sometimes as 'David versus Goliath', sometimes as 'big fat profiteers ruining the environment', and often as 'companies that collude together to swindle the public'. They all rely for their raw information on tips from members of the public and single-issue lobby groups with an axe to grind. They then conduct a clandestine investigation to obtain internal and external documents to form evidence against you.

Your crisis plan should include an early warning system to alert you that such an investigation is under way. Without early intelligence, it is difficult to avoid having to put together some sort of hurried defence.

If you are asked to do an interview for such a programme, we urge you always to take the opportunity since a well-trained spokesperson can do much to alleviate whatever damage the programme is trying to inflict.

Special care needs to be taken with investigative programmes that are oriented more towards entertainment than news and current affairs. Such programmes may not necessarily feel obliged under the 'fairness doctrine' to give you a decent chance of reply, and the audience will have been conditioned to see you as the villain.

If you do become aware of an investigative programme being made about you, our advice is to call in expert help immediately.

LEARNING POINTS

- Make sure that you are in control of media information.
- Make sure that it is accurate and up-to-date.
- Find out what the journalist's deadlines are.
- Always return calls.
- Be confident, open and friendly.
- Always correct misleading or inaccurate reporting.
- Prepare all key messages and examples.
- Get a clear picture of the item being prepared.
- Obtain broadcasting requests in writing.
- News agencies are the fastest way to access news organizations.
- The regional daily press are a priority.
- Be prepared for 24-hour media operations.
- Call in help to deal with investigative programmes.

8 Single-issue lobby groups

Single-issue lobby groups, also known as SILOs, are often the cause of a crisis breaking around the head of an organization when it least expects it. Your crisis team should become familiar with their methods of operation, since it is often a failure to monitor their activities that results in an issue developing into a full-blown negative story against you.

How does a SILO come about?

It is usually a group of likeminded campaigners who believe that they have an issue, currently being ignored, that deserves a higher public profile. It is often made up of people who have become frustrated by their lack of success in bringing the issue to the notice of politicians and other decision-makers. Sometimes they have tried to protest directly to a company or organization but have been rebuffed. As a result they tend to organize a campaign committee that has two initial objectives: to attract new members and raise funds for the cause. If that is successful, they often bring in professional help in the form of people who are not necessarily part of the campaign but who have experience in lobbying, advertising and marketing, and public relations. It is at this stage that anyone who might be targeted by the campaign should swing into action and monitor what is going on.

The SILO will almost certainly embark on an intelligence-gathering mission of its own to find key personnel who will brief them, to raid academic or scientific sources to support their case and to secure documents to use as evidence.

Most effective SILOs are expert in presenting the resulting material in the most damaging and emotional light for immediate public consumption. They are also very effective in giving source data to support their main allegations. Their news releases, for example, will often put their case in an eyecatching way on the first page and have a second page devoted to additional background information with scientific references and background notes, along with contact details for interviews.

If your organization is one of those mentioned in their issue, it is vital to keep track of these releases and sources so that they can be rebutted as necessary. Most scientific arguments are finely balanced judgements, and conclusions are not always watertight. Learned professors and researchers are notorious for disagreeing with each other's conclusions. The SILO will naturally select the evidence that is most beneficial to its case. You need to be as efficient in return, preferably with third-party endorsement.

Having gone for the maximum emotional impact, the campaign's next phase is usually to brief the media using highly trained and articulate spokespeople who are always available and who select their key messages and examples for high emotional impact. At the same time, and behind the scenes, their colleagues will be lobbying using techniques that we describe in the next chapter. When they sense that the dripfeed of media stories is getting attention and the decision-makers are beginning to take an interest, they often move up a gear and opt for highly visual TV, radio and press stunts to thrust the issue firmly in the public eye.

If the publicity stunts are successful, websites are used to provide back-up material, and the media start looking for more information and interviews.

If your organization is at the receiving end of such a campaign, you must be at least as well briefed as the media – so much so, that it is often productive to get one of your people to join the SILO as a member so that they can brief you on what is going on. Sympathetic journalists can also be recruited to report back on news conferences that the SILO has called to highlight an issue or an event.

The most important thing is to act quickly and decisively to spot holes in the group's arguments and the inaccuracies and distortions in what it is saying. It is also important to realize that, for a campaign to have been mounted in the first place, there must be a degree of support for the SILO's opinions. Consequently, responses from your spokespeople must be considered sympathetic and always make an effort to address the emotions underlying the issue. A strict rebuff on facts and figures will not be enough on its own.

You must always fight fire with fire.

Be open and honest, bearing in mind that the general public, whether they are members of the SILO or not, may be more supportive than you think, and it would be careless to needlessly denigrate their anxieties.

Some years ago, the media began to realize that they were being far too casual in accepting only the word of single-issue lobby groups. Allegations turned out to be untrue or misleading, and television, in particular, was accused of being seduced by the visual stunts and not by the legitimacy of the arguments. As a result, reporting procedures were tightened up and SILOs now have to work harder to convince journalists that they have a legitimate public-interest case.

Nevertheless, reporters can still be too easily seduced into taking a campaign message at face value. So, remember, broadcasters are obliged to balance their news and current affairs coverage and, if you are given the opportunity to air your case, seize the moment and make your voice heard. Do not, however, be tempted to do so in front of the opposition since the TV cameras and microphones will almost certainly pick up more of them than you.

We find it horrifying how often organizations will decide to 'keep a low profile' when a SILO begins to attack them. A firm, clear policy of rebuttal can often derail a campaign, particularly one based on half-truths. But if you allow it to gather steam and run unchallenged, it becomes a very dangerous beast indeed.

CASE STUDY 8.1
The environment

Greenpeace is one of the most powerful single-issue campaign groups in the world. It is highly organized and heavily funded by high-profile direct mailings, marketing, media campaigns and advertising. It was this organization, along with other environmental groups, who first brought toxic emissions, cancer-causing chemicals, save the whale and tuna, nuclear waste transportation and many other similar issues to mass attention.

The sheer scale and professionalism of Greenpeace's operations, headquartered in Holland, makes it a force to be reckoned with. It researches carefully, times its campaigns immaculately and organizes media stunts and briefings with extreme efficiency. It also makes mistakes but, such is the high approval rating for its activities, it is less negatively affected by lapses than most organizations.

Greenpeace's efficiency and potential for misleading public opinion came to the fore during the Shell/Brent Spar oil platform issue. Greenpeace had long been unhappy with the way in which oil companies had been allowed to carve up North Sea operations without committing themselves to the 'proper' disposal of rigs, platforms and other paraphernalia when operations came to an end.

As we saw in Chapter 4, Shell gathered the necessary scientific evidence to back up the case for burying the Brent Spar platform at sea. However, instead of carefully preparing decision-makers, the media and the general public for the news, the company more or less announced it out of the blue.

Greenpeace was quick to seize the initiative. It despatched its vessel, *Rainbow Warrior*, to the platform site. It sent its own camera team and invited the world's broadcasters and press to witness the boarding and 'capture' of the Brent Spar platform. It also made a series of claims about the toxic nature of the platform's contents which turned out to be untrue – but no one really noticed at the time. It was far more interesting to see a SILO in full cry against one of the richest oil companies in the world.

The imagery was clear: Shell was going to toss a huge lump of waste metal containing God knows what chemical and other detritus into the North Sea much as a lout would throw a beer can into the village pond.

The rest has made corporate communications and crisis management history.

Shell succeeded in getting the political support of the government. Indeed, Prime Minister John Major told the House of Commons that he had been assured by Shell that this was the most environmentally suitable option and that the company had his blessing.

But events were running so fast that, no sooner were the words out of his mouth than Shell had performed a massive about-turn.

Shell's board of directors in Holland had been watching the mounting bad publicity and the negative effect on worldwide petrol sales. They were particularly alarmed to see the losses sustained in some of their most environmentally sensitive countries such as Germany and the UK. On the very day that Mr Major was giving them the green light for a burial at sea, the board ordered Shell UK to reverse the decision and to promise further research.

Brent Spar has now been converted into a kind of pier in Finland and the estimated additional costs have been put at least £70 million – about double what it would have taken to follow the original plan.

CASE STUDY 8.2
Animal rights

Activists on this issue have been operational for many years, harassing laboratories that use animals for testing chemicals prior to their use in pharmaceuticals or cosmetic products.

More recently, they have seen the effect of their campaigning on companies that have cut back on the amount of animal testing they commission. This has been as a direct result of pressure from their customers and staff in the light of media campaigns.

Some companies say they are still forced by the regulators to test on animals before they are tried on human beings. The activists counter that, if products are so potentially dangerous that they have to be used on animals first, then they should not be made at all.

It is an ideological stand-off that is not going to be resolved in any immediate future.

Such is the emotion behind the issue that the staff and families of at least one major international company trading in cosmetic products has been physically threatened despite the fact that the organization has not been testing on animals for almost a decade.

Interestingly, the scientists within the cosmetics industry have been ingeniously inventing types of artificial skin and other substitutes that do not require animal testing. That, in itself, is testimony to the powerful arguments that the animal rights campaigners have managed to thrust into the public consciousness.

It is also a good example of companies watching for 'simmering' crises and acting accordingly. Few are naïve enough to think that they would have stopped testing without the actions of a single-issue lobby group. The relatively small groups that worked on the animal rights issue have now been joined by more powerful campaigns that have widened the scope around concerns about animals.

Compassion in World Farming has organized mass demonstrations, lobby campaigns and publicity events to highlight what they see as the mistreatment of farm animals.

They were particularly effective in drawing attention to the conditions endured by young lambs being exported to France. The police were put into the impossible position of holding back demonstrators and allowing overcrowded lorry loads of fluffy lambs to be driven on to ferries. The vehicles were slowed long enough for harrowing television pictures to be taken and, in one incident, a demonstrator died under the wheels of a truck. For a while, exporters were forced into spending considerable amounts of money flying the animals to France instead.

From a public relations perspective, one of the most powerful aspects of the Compassion in World Farming campaign was that their demonstrators were highly respectable people who said that they would never have dreamed of confronting the police over any other issue. In other words, they were not just a 'rent a mob', but ordinary people incensed by the way animals were treated.

The farmers, exporters, transporters and shipping companies appeared to be taken aback by the sheer weight of feeling and the organizational abilities of the campaign to get maximum publicity.

UNDERSTANDING CRISES AND THE THEORY OF COMMUNICATION

> With the exception of the police, the organizations concerned had never felt it necessary to undertake crisis planning monitoring to make sure that they knew what was in store for them.
>
> It is worth noting that the animal rights activists have now moved on and are concentrating on the use of genetically modified genes to increase the food supply. Some GM experiments require testing on animals, and the postbags of politicians and regulators are bulging as a result.

CASE STUDY 8.3
The disabled

Until recently, the interests of the disabled were represented by highly respectable, but rather worthy charity organizations. The deaf, the blind, wheelchair users, epilepsy sufferers, Downs syndrome family groups and many others raised funds for their causes and spent a proportion of it lobbying successive governments to improve conditions for the disabled.

The most obvious manifestation of these efforts is the much improved facilities for disabled people in public places. There has long been a suspicion among the lobby groups, however, that they are very much on the back-burner when it comes to the priorities of governments and MPs.

Slowly a coalition built up among the more activist members of disabled groups who took the view that discreet lobbying was not producing anything like the returns that they deserved. The only thing that decision-makers took notice of, they argued, was a high-profile and emotive campaign to ram the issues home. Writers covering the disabled found themselves being briefed by an altogether more militant group of spokespeople.

What was needed next was a catalytic event.

That came when the government let it be known that they were reviewing the whole issue of state support for the disabled. As with so many sectors of welfare state provision there was a complex and chaotic set of rules and regulations to judge what a disabled person is entitled to in terms of cash, allowances or physical support.

To the disabled groups, 'review' had to mean cutbacks to save treasury coffers. Their campaign message was that the government was so ruthless in its efforts to save money that it would rob the very people in society who had already been deprived of so much: their health and well-being.

They arranged, and were supported by, emotive media coverage and interviews with disabled people who demonstrated how much they stood to lose in benefits. They also were helped by several MPs in all parties who thought that the legislation review was going too far. Above all, they were helped by the literal bloodymindedness of some of the campaigners who broke through police lines and chained themselves to the railings (*à la* the women's rights activists of long ago) outside parliament and government offices.

They also decided on a macabre twist. As the police moved in, they covered themselves in blood-red paint. The resulting broadcast and press coverage of 'blood-covered' wheelchair occupants being hustled away by equally bloodstained police officers was a masterstroke in terms of a single-issue lobby group getting its message across.

Whenever disabled legislation comes up for discussion, those pictures are faithfully replayed and will be for years to come.

The important thing to remember is that the demonstration did not just happen. The campaign coalition had spent considerable time, money and effort to prepare public opinion for their outrageous action. The SILO was saying: 'Society is covered in the blood of our sacrifice and we are as capable as anyone else in expressing outrage that a government can attempt to put financial considerations before our welfare.'

As a result of all this a 'review' of the review was hastily announced.

LEARNING POINTS

- Monitor all SILO activity against you.
- Prepare rebuttal material and third-party endorsements.
- Find out what they are planning to do, and how.
- Research whether they are making an impact, and why.
- Have spokespeople and background information readily at hand.
- Recruit intelligence-gatherers.
- Watch out for publicity stunts.
- Try to 'get ahead' of an issue and stay there.
- Always address the concerns and emotions behind any issue.

9 Lobbying

In a 'sudden' or 'simmering' crisis you may well have to consider bringing in outside experts who specialize in what is colloquially known as 'lobbying'. The more accurate term is public affairs consultants, and most large companies or organizations have their own in-house capability that usually reports to the communications director. Small and medium-sized firms probably find it more cost-effective to bring in outside consultants on a project basis as and when needed.

These public affairs consultancy companies have been through a torrid time in recent years thanks to the unethical behaviour of some rubbing off on the whole sector. Broadly, some practitioners have been caught using unfair influence on some politicians to the point where some MPs had to admit that they received cash payments in the interests of the companies that employed them as consultants. There have also been allegations about lavish hospitality and improper approaches to politicians and civil servants.

As a result, the rules have been tightened considerably and all MPs are now required to register all their connections with lobbying organizations.

The consultants themselves have formed a professional body called the Association of Professional Political Consultants and have drawn up a code of conduct in an attempt to stamp out inappropriate behaviour.

Interviewed by the magazine *PR Week* in 2001, the top public affairs practitioners in the UK were asked to give their views on the state of lobbying since efforts had been made to 'clean up' their profession. They were agreed on the following, although not in any order of preference:

- Because power is now more diffuse, a range of 'pressure points' need to be deployed, including elected parliamentarians, non-elected experts, civil servants, journalists, academics, non-Governmental organizations and local communities.
- The trick is always to make the subjects of the lobbying or advocacy think that the final outcome is their decision, having been skilfully led towards it.

- 'Old-fashioned' methods of communication still work well, particularly among politicians and civil servants. They like proper handwritten letters and bound specially-prepared reports.
- What is called 'the call-back factor' is also important. How good are you at getting decision-makers to return your calls and enter into a discussion regarding your client?

In a crisis, you may need to pursue an active public affairs effort, and there are various routes open to you.

LOCAL COUNCILS

If the issue is relatively local, a direct approach to councillors or their officials is the most obvious course of action. A direct letter or, preferably, a meeting to discuss the matter often works well, and you can turn such approaches into useful third-party endorsements if the issue becomes public. In our experience, local council officials are well versed in how to deal with confidential or sensitive information, but local councillors are less reliable. If they can see some political mileage in it for themselves, their discretion can often go out of the window.

Controversial planning or health, safety and environment issues can often be resolved by an initial 'unofficial' approach to see what the council attitude is likely to be so that you can make the 'official' application or request in the most powerful way. Council officials and their political masters or mistresses do not like to have things blow up in their faces without warning and woe betide a company or organization that tips off the media prior to talking to the local authority.

It is always a good idea to have someone within the organization who is in touch with local councillors or their staff and who makes sure that they are invited to functions whether there is a potential crisis or not. The more familiar they are with what you do, the more well disposed to you they are likely to be if problems arise. If there is a sudden event, such as a fire or damage to premises that attracts major local media interest, it will be those same local councillors who sit in judgement on your actions and, possibly, on an application to restore things.

COUNTY COUNCILS

All of the above applies to the larger councils and the metropolitan areas too. You will probably have to try harder to get attention but you certainly should make sure that they are on your community relations list.

They should also be integrated into your crisis plan.

Every county council has an emergency planning unit that is charged with maintaining what is called a Major Civil Emergency Plan. This is the county council equivalent to your own crisis plan and is usually supervised and updated by a senior official on a full-time basis. During the Cold War period these tended to be secret documents administered by shadowy figures who were instructed by the Home Office not to reveal the contents. When the veil was eventually lifted, these planners were revealed to be completely out of touch with real life. They had tended to rely on old wartime remedies that were old-fashioned, out-of-date and usually unworkable, not least because the documents were secret with a limited circulation and thus had a limited exposure to fresh ideas.

The modern approach is completely transparent and open to public scrutiny, except for those parts of the Plan that cover genuine national security issues and, often, the private telephone numbers and addresses of the participants.

As part of your own crisis planning it is useful to get hold of a copy of the county council document and follow its outline. Clearly, if there is something they ought to know about your own arrangements, they should be notified accordingly.

Production or storage facilities that are categorized as being of high risk under government environmental regulations will be included in the Major Civil Emergency Plan as a matter of course. It is worth checking exactly how that information is updated.

The county and metropolitan emergency planners hold regular practice sessions, often with computer simulations, and are usually quite willing to have observers along. It is useful for at least some members of your own crisis team to have seen for themselves the complexities of dealing with major civil emergencies such as air crashes, chemical disasters, severe weather and nuclear events – whether accidental or warlike. One county council Plan we have seen defines a major civil emergency as: 'Any event (happening with or without warning) causing (or threatening to cause) death, injury, damage to property or the environment, or disruption to the community, which, because of the scale of its effects cannot be dealt with by the Emergency Services and Local Authorities as part of their day-to-day activities.'

It is no tribute to the written word but it does encapsulate the essential elements of what a county council sees as its responsibilities.

In greater detail these include the following priorities:

a   The initial rescue and transport of large numbers of casualties.
b   The involvement of large numbers of people.
c   The handling of a large number of enquiries from the public and media.
d   The need for large scale combined resources of Emergency Services.

e   The mobilisation of the Emergency Services and support organisations to cater for the threat of death, serious injury or homelessness of a large number of people.

They anticipate a civil emergency as going through the following phases:

a   Initial response – action by Emergency Services.
b   Consolidation – ongoing action by emergency teams supported by local authorities and other agencies as required. Control and co-ordination provided by police.
c   Recovery – the period when life saving is complete and the area made safe, when the caring for those involved or affected continues and when repair work can begin.
d   Return to normality – action by all involved in the emergency to restore normal conditions, investigate the causes and circumstances of the incident, evaluate the costs incurred and recommend ways to reduce similar risks and improve responses in the future. (Hampshire County Council Emergency Plan 1999)

See Appendix 8 for more details of the county Plan.

CONSTITUENCY MPs

MPs normally hold surgeries at regular intervals, and their offices will tell you when and where. In our experience, most MPs see them as useful opportunities for picking up public opinion away from the hothouse of Westminster. They are, however, often poorly attended and so can offer a rare opportunity to have 'quality time' with your local MP that may not be available in London.

It is often a good idea to send an outline of the issue in advance so that they know exactly who you are. As a result, they may be able to help with a 'simmering' crisis or have a word in someone's ear about legislation that may be causing you concern.

MPs are incredibly busy, so do not use this method too often, but it is undoubtedly cheaper than bringing in consultants. Remember, too, that if an MP takes up an issue they are entitled under law to have civil service action and an official response. You do not have that luxury.

With the growing involvement in all things by the European Parliament and Commission, similar methods can be used with your MEP. They tend to be even busier than their UK counterparts because they spend so much time travelling but if your issue or crisis has a European dimension, it is an avenue worth pursuing.

WESTMINSTER PARLIAMENTARY LOBBYING

Parliamentary lobbying carries the most sensitivity, so it is well worth relying on the expertise of specialist consultants who are usually staffed by former political activists or civil servants who know their way around the parliamentary system.

Consultants to whom we have spoken deplore the activities of those who have brought lobbying into disrepute, but all of them are agreed on certain things.

First, effective lobbying, particularly in a crisis, is only achieved by fast and reliable access to the people who make the decisions. These may be people who do not have it in their job title, but do in fact pull the levers of power. Part of what you are buying from a lobbying company is their knowledge of exactly who these people are and how they operate. Even more importantly they know the people you should steer clear of.

Second, all agree that lobbying should be an open and honest operation to smooth legislation, fix loopholes or plug gaps. Lobbying consultants are, in effect, a 'route map' around government, making it easier to press your case.

In 1999 the Neill Commission on Standards in Public Life took a lingering look at how consultants work and have tidied up the rules considerably. It was found, for example, that it was totally unethical for a public affairs company to receive speeches or draft legislation in advance of publication. The *Observer* newspaper had conducted an investigation and found that at least one lobbying company had been given documents indicating that the chancellor of the exchequer was planning to hold public spending at a certain figure. It was pointed out that city traders and other financial entities could make millions with that sort of insider information.

There was no actual evidence that the material had been used improperly, but the public perception was awful. So was the public view of another type of lobbying – the £1 million donation by the head of Formula One Motor Racing, Bernie Ecclestone, to the Labour Party. When they were elected to government Labour announced that motor racing would be exempt from legislation putting limitations on tobacco advertising. This represented a clear break for Mr Ecclestone, and a rat was duly smelt. Even multimillionaires, it was pointed out, did not give £1 million away with no purpose. The government duly returned the money, and henceforth the sum of a million pounds became known in political circles as a 'Bernie'.

Again, there was no evidence of actual impropriety but rather the public perception of it. All of which proves, we hope, that great care must be taken in the selection and use of public affairs consultants. The media is always on the look-out for new examples of bad practice to expose.

One area of activity that is acceptable under the new code of ethics is company sponsorship of political events. This has become a major feature of party conferences in particular, but it is an expensive business and it is hard to quantify its effectiveness.

It is probably more effective to hire the right consultants, prepare the ground for a targeted campaign and hope for the best. (When we talk about expense, you can expect a professional lobbying company to charge you anything between

£5000 and £20 000 per month. If you are involved in mergers or acquisition issues, the top people will cost you £3000 per day.)

At the time of writing, the government is planning to try to depoliticize the whole subject by handing over authority for decision-making on mergers from the Department of Trade and Industry to a new Competition Authority. While this may make lobbying on these matters less direct, it is unlikely to affect the need for public relations consultants to work their magic.

LEARNING POINTS

- Try to turn local government personnel into reliable third-party endorsees.
- Try 'informal' approaches before 'formal'.
- Liaise with county or metropolitan councils on crisis management planning.
- Lobby constituency MPs through their surgery system.
- Try to use expert public affairs consultancies for direct parliamentary lobbying.
- Take care not to break codes of conduct or parliamentary/government rules.
- 'Old-fashioned' methods of communicating with politicians or civil servants still work.

10 The price of failure

The principles of crisis management planning should now be well established, so it is probably time to illustrate the importance of actually managing the crisis when it arises.

The most effective way to do that is to select a potpourri of corporate disasters over the recent years – crises that were not only serious in financial terms but also in the public perception of the companies or organizations which appear to have failed to appreciate the impact of their actions that led to the emergency in the first place.

It should be said that each of the organizations we feature here would have said, prior to the actual occurrence of the crisis, that it had procedures in place that should have prevented it.

Since those procedures clearly didn't work and the 'simmering' issue became 'sudden', we analyse the factors that contributed to the problem. We start with the father and mother of all corporate failures and one which most corporate affairs specialists agree epitomizes how *not* to deal with a crisis.

THE EXXON VALDEZ CRISIS

The 1989 oil spill off the Alaskan coast will forever be known as the '*Exxon Valdez* crisis'. On 23 March the 1000-foot tanker, the *Exxon Valdez*, carrying 53 million gallons of crude oil, went aground on Bligh Reef in Prince William Sound. Over some days 11 million gallons of oil contaminated 1500 miles of coastline, destroyed wildlife and jeopardized the incomes of about 34 000 Alaskan fishermen.

As if this was not a bad enough scenario for the oil company, Exxon, it also emerged that the captain was below decks nursing a hangover at the time of the accident. He had left an unqualified third mate in charge of the ship and the radar system had been turned off.

Worse still, the company admitted that they knew the captain had a drink problem, and it was later discovered that there had been clear warnings for ten months prior to the accident that there was not enough emergency equipment in the area to deal with a spill of this magnitude. The six main oil companies that operated in Alaska had set up emergency procedures but had then mislaid the equipment and decommissioned a barge that should have been on permanent standby.

What made it a particular corporate disaster for Exxon, however, was the way in which the company handled the immediate aftermath. They were slow to react, and almost a whole day passed before the first company personnel arrived at the scene. The company chairman, Lawrence Rawl, was openly hostile to the media which was already building up a head of steam about the inadequacy of Exxon's response. It took him three weeks to get round to visiting the site to see for himself the damage that had been done to Alaska and, in the meantime, he tried to blame the Alaskan authorities and the coastguard service for not doing enough in terms of cleaning up.

As a result, to the media, Exxon could do nothing right, and its customers turned on it. Nearly 20 000 credit card holders sent their cards back to the company in protest.

In the end, Exxon was ordered to pay $5 million in punitive damages and its public reputation has never fully recovered, although it is still one of the largest oil companies in the world.

CRUCIAL FACTORS THAT TURNED THE INCIDENT INTO A CRISIS

1. The company incorporated their identity in the name of the ship making the situation, in public relations terms, worse than it otherwise would have been. 'A ship owned and operated by Exxon' is not as damaging as the '*Exxon Valdez* Disaster Ship'. Very few oil or chemical companies have ships named after them any more.
2. The company failed to appreciate warnings about the lack of equipment and resources to deal with an emergency spill. If it had made some attempt to liaise with other oil companies in the area and get them to contribute equipment, personnel and expertise, it may have helped deflect some of the media criticism from itself when a spill actually occurred.
3. The company failed to tackle the captain's drink problem and the training requirements of those under him.
4. It was slow to act when news of the accident broke.

5. It failed to properly monitor the media coverage and so did not recognize that it had a serious public relations problem over and above the accident itself.
6. Exxon's senior management was perceived to behave arrogantly.
7. There was insufficient appreciation that, in oil spill situations, 'emotion' always takes precedence over 'science'. The sight of fishermen and their families in trouble and wildlife dying in front of the cameras cannot be dealt with by buck-passing or technical arguments.
8. We also understand – and this is very common in these types of situation – that the management was persuaded by its lawyers to say as little as possible because of pending compensation payments. Crises often set the legal profession against public relations but, in this case, it has been more or less conclusively proved that the financial damage to Exxon's reputation was worse than any amount of compensation that could ever be imposed.

MONSANTO AND GM FOOD

For years the agro-chemical division of Monsanto, the American-owned chemical company, had been combining genetics research and molecular design to provide drugs and crops of a hybrid design. Food modified by these techniques had been on supermarket shelves in the United States for many years, and there had been little protest. The company convinced itself that the science was right and that their project was a commercial success.

The problems began to mount when the company started to export its GM crops to Europe, and it quickly became obvious that 'tampering' with food was an altogether more sensitive subject in countries that had suffered from a series of scandals involving the so-called 'food chain'.

The crisis was exacerbated by becoming an issue of 'choice'. Was the consumer being allowed to choose between using genetically modified products or not? 'No,' said Monsanto and the other companies involved. Monsanto's mistake was to take the high ground and mount an aggressive public relations campaign extolling the virtues of GM crops. Apparently blind to public opinion, the company continued to dig its heels in and only realized its mistake when the major supermarkets and international food companies bowed to pressure from their customers to drop GM products.

The cost to the company was catastrophic, and millions were lost in turnover and share price. As a result, it was forced to merge with another company, and there was even talk of selling off the agro-chemical business altogether.

CRUCIAL FACTORS THAT TURNED THE SITUATION INTO A CRISIS

1. Monsanto's senior management thought that it had the science right but failed to take into account the emotional fears of the public.
2. The management convinced itself that what had worked in the United States would transfer unproblematically to Europe and other parts of the world.
3. The company was already perceived to be secretive and therefore had no reservoir of goodwill with the media and other audiences when an outcry arose.
4. A high-profile advertising campaign backfired because it gave the impression that the company was overbearing and unwilling to listen.
5. The company failed to recognize that the public was unwilling to take risks with food for little benefit to themselves. (One of the key planks of the company's argument was that GM crops would be good for the farmers of the developing world.) The public took that to be a naked commercial ploy to control crop supplies to the poorest countries in the world.
6. We have been told, but cannot prove, that the public was not impressed by the fact that the leading company spokesperson in Europe was an American. He became the public face of GM crops, and the audiences did not like it.

ALLIED DOMECQ

One of the world's largest owner of branded alcoholic drinks, Allied Domecq, based in the UK, made a strategic decision to sell 3500 public houses that it owned and operated.

It announced in the media that it had agreed a £2.4 million 'full and fair' offer from a rival public house operator, the brewing company Whitbread.

The deal was referred to the Government Competition Commission, but everyone seemed to be agreed that the deal was 'certain to go through'. However, Allied Domecq was apparently completely unaware that there was another company interested in their pubs. Punch Taverns announced that it would like to come in at a higher level and was prepared to go as high as £2.94 million although that figure was later revised downwards to £2.72 million. This was £300 000 more than the board had agreed with Whitbread.

The ensuing battle played out over several weeks and the news headlines were awful, the whole affair being dubbed 'A Comedy of Errors'.

Sir Christopher Hogg, a hitherto much respected businessman had been brought in as Allied Domecq's chairman, but compounded the problems by trying to blame media coverage for the mess.

Analysts pointed out to journalists that, in their opinion, Sir Christopher had inherited a chaotic management system in the first place and the bungled sale was a direct result of their incompetence. An extraordinary shareholders' meeting was held during which the boards' actions were described as 'deplorable' and 'completely stupid'.

The shareholders were not the only ones to be unhappy. Whitbread had been made to look stupid and had lost its chance of owning the pubs, and Punch Taverns had been forced to spend more on advisory fees than it otherwise would have done.

The greatest loser was Allied Domecq itself. It not only lost the chance of capitalizing on a higher bid, it also lost the confidence of its own shareholders and the City. In addition, the company was forced to pay a staggering £40 million in fees to advisers, banks and lawyers.

CRUCIAL FACTORS THAT TURNED THE SITUATION INTO A CRISIS

1. The board and its new chairman did not ask themselves a simple question: could there be another bidder in the pipeline?
2. Having failed to do this, they gave the impression, in their public announcement, that the whole deal had been stitched up by the 'old brewery boy network'.
3. When the worms came out of the can, the company tried to brazen it out and blame others, seemingly oblivious to the concerns of its shareholders. As a result, Allied Domecq lost control of the situation and plunged into a full-blown crisis.

BARINGS

A large advertisement appeared in most national and international newspapers in May 1998. It contained lots of legal words but the headline said it all: 'We announce the liquidation of Barings Plc in the High Court of London, Chancery Division.' It was the formal end of a company that had been established by Sir Francis Baring in 1762.

Barings had attained the status of a respected world bank through handling, among other things, France's war reparations after the Battle of Waterloo, acting as agents for the United States and Imperial Russia, and issuing bonds for both China and Japan.

The liquidation was a direct consequence of the fact that the bank had collapsed with £660 million of debts thanks to the actions of one of its foreign exchange dealers working on Simex – the Singapore Money Exchange.

The English-born trader, Nick Leeson, had got into the habit of burying any trading losses into a special account numbered 88888. Like many gamblers, he tried to conceal losses in the hope that he could falsely account future gains and use the surpluses to secretly pay off the hidden debts.

Over two years, £850 million of the bank's money disappeared and he was subsequently imprisoned for his actions. Barings Bank went into liquidation and was eventually paid just £1 by a Dutch bank for its non-liquid assets.

Despite being part of what is hailed as one of the most heavily regulated sectors in the world, this bank had so few checks and balances to monitor the activities of its traders and executives that Leeson had been able to put the fortunes of the entire enterprise into jeopardy. Barings, for example, allowed him to trade upfront and balance his own books (the back office function) with no oversight. Because he appeared to be making so much money for the bank, his line managers allowed him to get on with his job unsupervised as long as bonuses were maintained. The subsequent crisis led to the destruction of the bank, huge financial burdens for its bond-holders and investors, 1200 job losses and a trader in prison.

Perhaps the only positive thing to come out of the whole episode was a new piece of government regulation that set up the Financial Services Authority – a body that now has the power to police banks, no matter how well established, and ensure that they comply with all national and international rules and principles.

CRUCIAL FACTORS THAT TURNED THE SITUATION INTO A CRISIS

1. The company had a management with a family history which encouraged a refusal to accept that something so horrific could happen. They were not trained to look for the 'simmering' crisis.
2. The management appeared to have paid no more than lip service to international banking rules specifying that you should separate the 'front' office function from the 'back' office function.
3. There appears to have been encouragement for a 'gung ho' culture in which traders were allowed to feel so powerful that they turned themselves into gamblers in the belief that they could spend their way out of trouble as long as the management kept out of the way. Greed also played its part. Senior managers did not want to put their own bonuses in jeopardy.
4. There did not appear to be a crisis management exercise in place to deal with fraud, money-laundering and financial collapse anywhere in the world, let alone with something perpetrated by a member of the company's own staff.

NATO IN KOSOVO – A CRISIS REVERSED

In March 1999 the Supreme Allied Command Europe (SHAPE) was instructed by NATO to undertake bombing missions against Serbian targets in retaliation for their ill-treatment of Kosovo Albanians. It was painfully obvious, soon after the campaign started, that the SHAPE–NATO communications system was in no fit condition to cope with either the demands for information on the bombing or the misinformation being disseminated by the Serbs.

NATO had a widely respected spokesperson in Jamie Shea but he was clearly not totally 'in the loop'. During conflicts the military are notoriously reluctant to give information. Most commanders of all nationalities are content with the doctrine 'We will only tell them things when we have won'. They fail to realize that, nowadays, military campaigns can only be sustained politically if the voting public know what is going on.

The situation in Kosovo came to a head when the American General, Wesley Clark, accused the Serbs of bombing their own civilian convoys. It was a totally untrue allegation and the media began to lose confidence in everything the military were saying. They became even more suspicious when American commanders brought, to a news conference, a videotape which they claimed to show one convoy incident when, in fact, it was another.

The British government watched the unravelling communications crisis with growing horror. The prime minister, Tony Blair, despatched his press spokesperson Alistair Campbell to try to sort things out. The two had always worked closely on media-handling and they knew what to do in a crisis.

Campbell set up a Media Operations Centre and called upon NATO governments to send their 'brightest and best' communicators to participate. He said later that he insisted that the media effort should consist of four elements:

- *Rebuttal*: identifying and responding to Serb information.
- *Lines*: catchy phrases for spokespeople to use.
- *Talking heads*: ghosted articles from senior NATO leaders to appear in newspapers and magazines.
- *The grid*: twice-daily conference calls between Brussels (SHAPE headquarters) and key national capitals to coordinate diaries and messages for the national leaders to make sure that they were all saying the same things.

These actions significantly improved the NATO communications system and, as a result, the political leadership of the Western world regained the initiative.

BRITISH AIRPORTS AUTHORITY – A SUCCESS STORY

All the case studies so far have described the price of failure in terms of lost business, lost reputation or lost credibility, or a combination of any of these. Here is one which presents a success story.

Mindful that, in the airport business, the price of failure can be very high indeed, the British Airports Authority decided to introduce a management system that put dedication to customer satisfaction at its heart. It principally involves the management of information.

The most obvious manifestation of this system is the men and women with clipboards who interview incoming customers while they are waiting for their baggage or outbound passengers waiting to check in.

What the interviewers are told is analysed and codified and, if a pattern of concern is noticed, it is reported immediately to the BAA board of directors.

Remedial action is then identified and the matter resolved where possible.

The BAA management says that it regards this information-gathering system as a vital tool for spotting 'simmering' crises. It protects their brand image, and it has worked elsewhere. It is a formula that BAA now sells to other airports abroad.

Part II

Practical Crisis Communication

11 Practical steps to prepare for a crisis

As we discussed in Part I, preparation and common sense are a central theme of crisis management. Both are made easier if members of your organization make it second nature to ask questions and monitor for unusual or undesirable occurrences.

For example, is a news reporter making enquiries about a matter that does not seem to make any sense? Don't just ignore the matter and hope that it will go away. It might. But, just as likely, it will be a signal of a 'simmering' problem that needs to be dealt with. There will always be false alarms but the practice of analysing the importance of an apparently trivial issue is good in itself. It is, however, crucial that your response to a situation is measured and in keeping with its importance. Some organizations have been known to overreact and make a situation worse than it started out.

This is where the crisis team comes in. Like so many task forces created within an organization, this one must have a clear role, well-defined powers and, above all, someone chairing it who is either at the top of the management structure or with clear communications lines to those who are.

To be clear what we mean. An international company might have three production centres and a European headquarters based in Britain. Each plant should have a crisis plan and action groups to deal with local events chaired, probably, by the plant manager. For this plan to work effectively, he must have an open channel to the UK managing director who, in turn, should have a crisis committee for dealing with anything negative in the UK. That MD must have an open line to the senior management and their crisis team at world headquarters.

You will notice that we have deliberately used the word 'should'. Many readers might be amazed to learn how many leading international companies are hard-pressed to demonstrate that they have such a system in place, let alone that it works when necessary. To be fair to those managers who have not planned for a crisis, this area of work is a 'non-profit' function of the system and can be costly if it is not done properly – costly, not only in terms of management time, but also in terms of putting in place the technology to make sure that it works under fire.

The composition of a crisis team is difficult to talk about in abstract terms because organizations have different needs (see 'The Crisis Team', Chapter 14) but some general points do apply. Apart from having a powerful chairperson, it must also have a designated deputy. Negative events have a habit of arising at night, at the weekend and usually a bank holiday. They also tend to happen when the chairperson of the crisis team has decided to go on a course, attend a conference or is stuck in hospital as a result of a car crash.

The same could be said for each of the other members of the team, so it is always worth nominating a deputy for each function. Do not, however, just name a deputy and hope that nothing happens. Substitute crisis team members must know as much as their boss and must be copied in on everything that might be relevant. Regular meetings and practice sessions should include them even if they cannot all attend because of the pressure of other matters, like running the business.

Our advice is to make sure that each of the following crucial functions of a business is covered:

- legal (company secretary or retained lawyer)
- human resources
- operations
- quality control
- corporate affairs (in-house, consultancy or both)
- information technology.

Distribution, marketing sales, plant management, transport, the director of finance or head of treasury are other possibilities, depending on the nature and extent of the potential issues.

Crucial to the success of this group is the selection of a spokesperson who, with a deputy, is privy to everything that is known about the crisis issue. Nothing must be kept secret or fudged. That is not because you want to reveal to outsiders all your secrets but because the spokesperson needs to know where the sensitive areas are and prepare answers to any questions that may arise. It will be part of their job to put together a question-and-answer document at very short notice. The point at which the crisis is unfolding is no time to discover that they have been left in the dark and have only found out about it in the city pages of the national press.

A question-and-answer document must be carefully prepared and updated using what we call the 'unpeeling the onion' method. Ask yourself a crucial question that might come up during a crisis and give your considered response. Then say to yourself or your team: 'What happens if they then ask me...?' You

PRACTICAL STEPS TO PREPARE FOR A CRISIS

will need to unpeel several layers of the onion before you will be able to feel relaxed about answers to that line of enquiry. We have often seen spokespeople stumped when a perfectly obvious follow-up question has been posed but the answer has not been rehearsed in advance.

A note, here, about the confidentiality of question-and-answer documents. Make sure that the print run is limited and that each copy is numbered and signed for. Without these precautions they have a nasty habit of going 'walkabout', and some have even fallen into the hands of journalists who take great delight in knowing how much trouble you have gone to in advance to second-guess them. This is not to say that we believe in the art of falsifying responses or trying to mislead journalists. It is simply that there is usually a reason for something having been done in a certain way and you are entitled to articulate that fact confidently if you are asked about it under stressful circumstances. It must be emphasized that 'killer facts' are the best part of a spokesperson's armoury. Falsehoods, prevarication and being 'sparing with the *actualité*' are not acceptable. The laws of libel prevent us from selecting examples from the political world and the civil service in recent years, but the list is endless. The truth of the matter is that a journalist will see through the evasions in a nanosecond if their own sources of information are any good.

The spokesperson's job is made immeasurably easier if he or she is backed up by a confident team who are well prepared to deal with the unexpected. We have a test question when we are called in to look at the communications aspect of a crisis plan: 'After the emergency services (in the case of an accident or disaster) who should be contacted first?' World headquarters is one answer. The managing director or the head of the crisis team is another. God is another. The *real* answer is 'As many telephonists or receptionists that you have ever employed.' It is they, after all, who are the leading face of the organization, and it is the communications systems that come under pressure first. You should budget to train telephonists and receptionists in how to deal with the variety of incoming calls. How should they deal with the media, staff, customers and clients? They must also know how to cope well with potential third-party endorsees – for example, the local councillor who sits on the local planning committee and wants to know why your factory has just blown up. Or the MD of the office next door who is anxious for a similar explanation. If they are given the brush-off they will not be of much help when you want permission to rebuild.

If your organization employs security guards, the same applies. We always have considerable sympathy with the gatehouse guard who is suddenly faced with a pack of hungry journalists with tape recorders, microphones and television cameras. Without training, the natural reaction is to put one hand over the lens, tell the assembled group that they are trespassing and that they will be arrested at the earliest opportunity. We were once much amused to see an investigative television team turn up at the headquarters of a company whose managing director's luxurious home had also been filmed. The TV company had with them a group of protesters from Wales who were objecting to the building of a waste incinerator. When they knocked on the door of main reception, they were faced with a security guard who they asked for access to conduct an interview with a member of the management. The guard disappeared for a while only to return with the hilarious reposte: 'I have been told to tell you that there is no one here!' It was not the guard's fault. It was the fault of the company for not having thought through the consequences of a camera team turning up out of the blue. In the case of a contentious sector, like waste management, you would have thought that it would have been one of its top priorities.

To avoid slip-ups like this, it is worth, at some stage during the selection of a crisis team and agreeing their roles, to bring in crisis management advisers. This can be done on a retained or consultancy basis and is valuable because someone who is not directly employed by the company is usually better placed to spot the potential problems and work out how they can be dealt with. Regular updating and practice must be built into the crisis budget bearing in mind that, whatever business you may be in, nothing ever stands still – not least in terms of staff turnover and the acquisition or disposal of businesses.

Once the team is in place it should be one of their priorities to set up what the White House in Washington calls the 'situation room'. Without being over-dramatic, this is a place where the crisis team can meet in confidence (see Appendix 1, 'The Crisis Centre' for details). It must be equipped with everything that might be needed in an emergency – databases with crisis management software, extra telephones, PCs, TV, radio, videos, background briefing materials, maps and charts. Everything – down to stationery, flipcharts and tea and coffee machines.

The next priority is to set an exercise to make sure that it all works. An oil company once simulated a disaster involving one of their tankers at sea only to discover that both the internal and external communications systems collapsed completely. They would have been utterly paralysed in the event of such an emergency happening in real life. Having said all this, an effective crisis plan must not be so complicated that no one can understand or implement it under pressure. By all means print a limited edition of your plan but also have a simplified guide handy. Most crisis plans we see are great as doorstops or for reaching the top bookshelf but are far too difficult to follow under crisis conditions. Remember, too, that the crisis probably only became one because evidence of its imminent arrival was ignored. Analysis of the Japanese attack on Pearl Harbour revealed that the American government had received more than enough information to take precautions to protect its fleet. They failed to do so because the intelligence was spread around so many places – the State

Department, the Pentagon and elsewhere. The collation process failed. Nonetheless, it could be argued that ultimately this turned out to be for the greater good of the world since the attack persuaded the United States that it must become more fully engaged in the Second World War.

It is reported, but never to our knowledge confirmed, that if the Duke of Edinburgh heard that a particular news organization was planning to do a negative story about him he would get someone to tip off the Press Association news agency. By doing so, it was calculated, it became less of an exclusive and, therefore, less dramatic and valuable. Some companies that regularly attract negative publicity issue news releases about absolutely anything that happens out of the ordinary. It is a ploy to condition news editors into thinking 'Oh no, not them again' – a tactic that is only for the really bold!

LEARNING POINTS

- ◆ A crisis team and operational centre must be ready at all times.
- ◆ Monitoring issues, events and coverage is vital.
- ◆ The spokesperson must be a central ingredient.
- ◆ Always rehearse questions and answers and make them accurate.
- ◆ Practise the crisis plan at all levels.
- ◆ Employ or retain crisis experts.
- ◆ Do not make the planning too complicated.

12 Internal audiences

In our experience, those companies that communicate best internally tend to do as well externally and, in doing so, have a higher reputation in the eyes of their outside audiences.

In a crisis, however, the free flow of information will either have to be enhanced or, in some circumstances, restricted. Again, it is only by planning in advance and by having a prearranged procedure in place that things will work effectively under fire.

Internal communications are vital ingredients in the process of spotting a looming or 'simmering' situation. Internal e-mail or an Intranet site are the most obvious means by which members of staff can alert management about issues that may need dealing with.

Internal publications can also be utilized for this purpose, with members of staff being given anonymity if necessary. The in-house magazine is also a good forum for making staff aware of the outlines of a crisis plan and their part in it. If there is a staff appraisal system in place, there should always be an item on the agenda dealing with under-the-surface issues that concern the individual. The human resources department needs to build a fast-track routing system for what comes out of those appraisals to the person who chairs the crisis team. It should be his or her judgement, in consultation with the deputy, as to whether the information is important enough to warrant the calling together of the crisis team or whether it should more properly be dealt with using the usual HR procedures.

It is worth noting that, in recent times, the whole issue of 'whistle-blowing' within an organization has become an important topic for senior managers to address. When it has been badly handled it has become a crisis in itself. So much so that there is now legislation in the UK (the Public Interest Disclosure Act 1998) to protect individuals who have found themselves victimized as a result of 'whistle-blowing' about a scandal brewing within an organization or reporting an individual for misconduct.

In any case, it is never wise to alienate a whistle-blower since they may feel that their only recourse is to approach someone else who is willing to listen and take the matter seriously. That someone is often a journalist or someone with access to the media and, when it gets to that point, the issue has run out of your control. Tempting as it is to brand someone a troublemaker, it is often more shrewd to think of them as being helpful. It is also advisable to include an outside party to consider the issues brought to you by a whistle-blower. If they come out into the open at a later date, the outsider can be used as a key third-party endorsee to testify about how seriously you took the matter.

We do not recommend that all members of staff receive a copy of the crisis plan since its circulation should be restricted to the crisis team who have to activate it. It may, however, be useful to distribute a précis of the plan with the pack of information given to all new employees. This will demonstrate that you take emergencies seriously and that you want their full participation.

There is an interesting psychological point about having a workforce fully briefed on crisis measures: if they are trained to think about dealing with the unexpected in a positive way there is more likelihood that they will do it well.

One of the key factors in dealing with a crisis is that you circumnavigate usual procedures and call on people to use their common sense and judgement. You are, in effect, giving people an authority to act that they would not normally have. An emergency is no time to have everything referred to a committee for decision.

It is very important that the crisis plan includes exact measures to make sure that the affected workforce and other parts of the company know what has happened and how it is being dealt with. The staff are a crucial link between the organization and external audiences and it should go without saying that all internal messages should complement, if not match, those being given externally. If they don't, confusion ensues and where there is confusion there is doubt about the control being exercised by management.

Those working for you should always give the impression that they are working for an open company. Should a journalist approach them for information, for example, they should be told to find out as much as possible about the journalist and his or her publication and then report the approach to the person with responsibility for dealing with corporate affairs. Members of staff must be told never to say to a journalist such things as 'No comment' or 'We are sworn to secrecy and only the company spokesperson is allowed to talk to the media.' It gives the immediate impression that the company is secretive and has something to hide. It may even encourage the journalist to go to other sources of information that may not be to your advantage.

On the other hand, you do not want all members of staff to think that they can each be a spokesperson for the company. That leads to confusion and lack of control. During a crisis someone should be delegated to keep open the channels of internal communication and, if necessary, hold regular briefings. There is no more sure way of upsetting the workforce than letting them find out important things from outside sources. The briefings can, in themselves, be important forums for obtaining feedback from staff and for reinforcing the message that they need to be careful about what they say to external audiences. A final point about internal communications in a crisis. Always remember that the people who are most vulnerable are those at the lowest point of the totempole – those people who it is all too easy to forget to brief. As former journalists, we know the value of chatting up contract cleaners, security people, receptionists, drivers and telephone operators. If you fail to include these people in the crisis training you will regret it.

LEARNING POINTS

- Have a mechanism that opens up all internal communications channels.
- Encourage all staff to express their concerns.
- Do not brand a 'whistle-blower' a 'troublemaker'.
- Try to include an outside party when dealing with 'whistle-blower' information.
- Give all staff a précis of the crisis plan.
- Hold staff briefings during an emergency.
- Train personnel from top to bottom – especially the bottom.

13 The spokesperson

In a crisis the spokesperson is central to the entire operation. Whoever is selected to take on this role is the internal conduit who makes sure that information passes quickly and easily up and down the organization. The job also involves capturing the essence of what is happening and fashioning the messages for external consumption.

Most of the time, the spokesperson will be the public face of the organization but, on occasions, may also be responsible for bringing in other management figures to provide technical knowledge or details about what the strategy might be once the crisis is over. This would normally be the managing director in the case of a large corporation. In a small to medium-sized firm the managing director may be the actual spokesperson although this is not considered to be particularly wise since, in the face of the unexpected, the MD should be directing operations, not speaking about them.

The spokesperson must encourage other managers to seize the crisis as an opportunity rather than a disaster. They should make sure that each of them appreciates the need for honesty, openness, accessibility, empathy, compassion and to be proactive rather than defensive. All of this is something of a tall order in an emergency but is achievable given the sort of planning we have talked about. (See 'Spokesperson' in Appendix 2.)

PLANNING

The spokesperson should make it their job to ensure that the crisis database is constantly updated with the necessary contact numbers of internal and external audiences. They are also responsible for preparing the easy-to-understand background briefing documents that can be immediately issued. These cover the background and history of the organization, what it does, how many people it employs and any other relevant information. They are also the custodian of up-to-date videos and a picture library.

Although this function will often fall to the head of human resources, the spokesperson should also be heavily involved in any crisis training that is being provided. This is valuable at several levels. It makes sure that the spokesperson knows what each individual is capable of, it allows them to be known to key personnel since it will be the spokesperson's job to brief them during a crisis and, lastly, it gives the spokesperson an overview of who does what and how. This will be a vital function if the media or others need to be given a picture of the company's organization.

Although this may be a job given to someone else, it also quite often falls to the spokesperson to identify third-party endorsees from other organizations. This is often done through the spokesperson's counterpart or directly. The key thing is to have a preselected group that the media and others can be referred to.

AS THE CRISIS GROWS

It is the job of the spokesperson to make sure that there is a 24-hour media centre opened as soon as possible whether the situation has reached the public or not. It is the task of that group to monitor progress of the situation and prepare news releases to be issued if and when necessary. Key journalists and their publications must be instantly available on the database.

If they are not already retained (which they should be), a public relations consultancy will probably need briefing and so will a media monitoring company. These days, it should be part of the process to monitor the Internet and the company Intranet as well.

If possible, a place where media briefings will be conducted should have been identified and activated (extra telephones, interview rooms, background briefing papers, company backdrop with logos and all necessary visual aids).

The main aim of all this activity is to ensure that, should the crisis go 'live', you are in a position to seize the initiative and establish yourself as the authoritative source for information. In a crisis every vacuum must be filled by you because, if you don't, someone else will.

The spokesperson must have the confidence to be as open as possible and to encourage total truthfulness. At the same time they must not speculate about things that are not yet clear. Any inaccurate or misleading information – whether in the media or elsewhere – must be corrected immediately. It will be the job of the spokesperson's team to log all outgoing information and actions to correct misinformation. An enquiry log should also be established (see Appendix 2). It should be the job of the spokesperson to brief all key personnel about how to handle enquiries and to ensure that any news releases which are sent out are copied to the necessary internal departments. This is not to turn everyone into mini-spokespeople but to make sure that everyone knows what is being said publicly.

If a news conference is required, the spokesperson should organize it. This task includes inviting guests, introducing speakers and providing all necessary materials and follow-up. It is as well to remind everyone who is taking part that there is no such thing as 'off the record'. Nor should anyone ever say 'No comment', because this is taken to mean 'guilty as charged'.

It is important that the spokesperson and their team are not just regarded as smooth front people. Those observing should see the communications function as integral to the whole operation. The attitude should be adopted that the organization has information to share rather than a position to defend. It is the spokesperson's attitude and body language that creates the impression rather than the words being used. This comes with good preparation, including rehearsal, and by describing complicated issues with simple words, illustrated by easy-to-understand examples.

Dr Cheryl Travers, a lecturer in organizational behaviour and human resource management at Loughborough University in the UK has identified eight well-documented defence mechanisms which people use to protect themselves in difficult situations. A designated spokesperson would do well to study and digest them (see Figure 13.1).

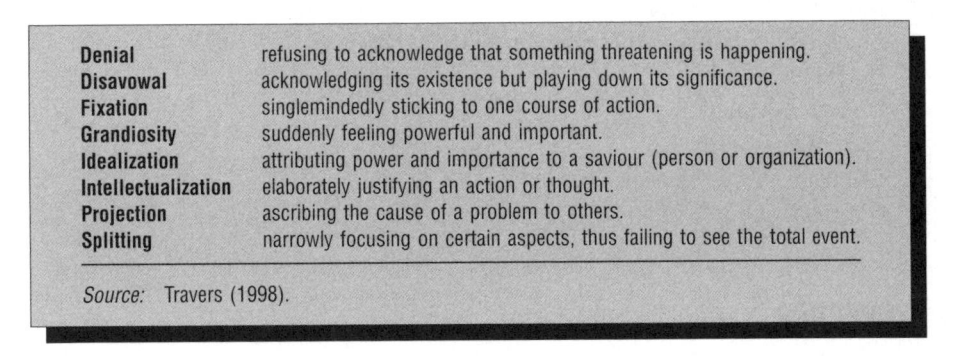

Denial	refusing to acknowledge that something threatening is happening.
Disavowal	acknowledging its existence but playing down its significance.
Fixation	singlemindedly sticking to one course of action.
Grandiosity	suddenly feeling powerful and important.
Idealization	attributing power and importance to a saviour (person or organization).
Intellectualization	elaborately justifying an action or thought.
Projection	ascribing the cause of a problem to others.
Splitting	narrowly focusing on certain aspects, thus failing to see the total event.

Source: Travers (1998).

Figure 13.1 Defence mechanisms in a crisis

AFTER THE CRISIS

The spokesperson will play a vital role in the aftermath, particularly if there are public inquiries to be held and a continuing interest in the company or organization and how it is recovering. Internal analysis will have to be undertaken to see how well communications worked, and there will be detailed effort needed to monitor how the external audiences were kept informed. Negative and positive feedback needs to be encouraged and it is often the job of the spokesperson to get it and feed it into the crisis planning matrix. There has never been a crisis yet where everything worked perfectly but learning from the experience must be taken seriously.

One essential question to ask in any inquest is 'Were we flexible enough?' In our experience, crisis plans tend to be too rigid when something actually happens. Using common sense and throwing out a nonsensical bit of the plan demonstrates true flexibility.

LEARNING POINTS

- Be responsible for all communications and messages.
- Seize the crisis as an opportunity.
- Instill the need for honesty, openness, accessibility, empathy, compassion and proactivity.
- Create and update the crisis database.
- Prepare and update briefing materials.
- Be involved in training.
- Identify third-party endorsees.
- Create a 24-hour media centre.
- Monitor all communications.
- Establish yourself as the sole authoratative source.
- Do fill vacuums.
- Do not speculate.
- Log all enquiries.
- Circulate news releases.
- Get feedback.

REFERENCE

Travers, Cheryl (1998), 'Handling the stress', in Michael Bland, *Communicating out of a Crisis*, London: Macmillan.

14 The crisis team

The crisis team should be made up of senior management with the authority to act quickly and decisively in the face of both 'sudden' and 'simmering' situations which could have a negative impact on the well-being of the company or organization. The exact composition will depend heavily on the type of operation you have, but the following set-up is applicable to most:

- Chairperson
- Deputy chairperson
- Human resources
- Finance
- Legal and insurance
- Communications
- Operations
- Health, safety and environment
- Record-keeper (preferably a senior PA or secretary).

The chairperson has a deputy but each of the other categories should also have someone else who is fully briefed on the roles and responsibilities they have in an emergency situation. These people must be included on the list of those who hold the crisis manual and computer disks, attend update meetings and take part in practice exercises.

Following is a summary of the roles of each member of the crisis team. See Appendix 1 for a checklist of duties for crisis team members.

THE ROLES OF EACH CRISIS TEAM MEMBER

CHAIRPERSON

- Selects a deputy and the team.

- Calls meetings and practice sessions.
- Acts as key contact with board of directors and executive management.

DEPUTY CHAIRPERSON

- Assumes all the duties and roles of an absent chairperson.
- Keeps in contact with all team members.
- Activates the crisis plan.
- Assigns roles.
- Utilizes resources.
- Takes responsibility for budgets.
- Activates supplier/client liaison.

HUMAN RESOURCES

- Manages all staffing issues.
- Takes responsibility for training requirements.
- Organizes shifts/overtime.
- Manages property and equipment requirements.
- Manages personnel files and contact numbers.

FINANCE

- Keeps the budget.
- Approves costs.
- Estimates the financial impact on the business.
- Liaises with shareholder interests.
- Maintains contact with banks and financial institutions.

LEGAL AND INSURANCE

- Manages access to all legal and insurance documents.
- Liaises with insurance companies, loss adjusters and assessors.
- Takes responsibility for regulatory notifications.
- Recruits additional legal advice.
- Assesses legal and insurance impact immediately and over time.
- Liaises with communications representative on internal and external comment.

COMMUNICATIONS

- Prepares background documents.
- Acts as spokesperson.
- Drafts news releases.
- Handles media enquiries.
- Appoints communications team.
- Monitors the media.
- Identifies external audiences.
- Develops key messages.

OPERATIONS

- Leads crisis operations team.
- Calls up additional technical support.
- Briefs outside contractors.
- Implements recovery programme.
- Budgets for replacement equipment and additional staff.

HEALTH, SAFETY AND ENVIRONMENT

- Takes responsibility for mandatory notifications to regulators.
- Notifies environment agencies.
- Liaises with local interest groups and authorities.
- Maintains contact with trade associations and other companies.
- Notifies in-house and external medical teams.

RECORD-KEEPER

- Drafts agendas.
- Notifies participants of meetings and action papers.
- Takes accurate notes of each meeting and decisions taken.
- Organizes additional secretarial or PA back-up.
- Supervises telephonists and receptionists.

THE ROLES OF THE CRISIS TEAM AS A WHOLE

This team, once appointed, has a number of roles that are defined as follows:

- preparation

- implementation
- practice
- action
- follow-up.

PREPARATION

Preparation includes the identification of issues and the consequence of each turning into a crisis. It also includes the compilation of lists of internal and external audiences who will need to be informed about what is going on and the drafting of background information for instant release in the case of an emergency. An early task will be to identify assembly points for staff, emergency services and the media. Where possible, these areas will be distant from each other since you will not want staff and media together – let alone all three. Assembly points are usually at gatehouses, car parks or recreational areas and should, ideally, have some accommodation with communications facilities. They must be marked (Assembly point A, B, C and so on) and included on any maps which may be included in the crisis plan. The team will also need to identify a location that can be equipped as a crisis room (with an off-site back-up should the emergency involve evacuation). See Appendix 1 for a checklist of what this room should contain.

IMPLEMENTATION

Implementation involves obtaining the necessary financial and other resources to be ready for use in a crisis. You identify these by drawing up scenarios that could lead to a crisis and analyse the possible consequences. What additional resources will be needed and what might the costs be? Should there be additional training, staffing, overtime or outside help? Will we need additional and specialist equipment?

PRACTICE

Practice includes the training of key personnel and the identification of weak areas of the plan. Regular meetings should be held to keep the crisis plan under review and, at least once a year, a simulation exercise should be held. This should be done with prior notification to avoid disruption of business, or without notification if that is appropriate. These practice sessions should involve the entire crisis team and their deputies along with selected personnel from outside who can bring a fresh eye to the preparations that have been made. Some companies include selected members of the media, outside consultants, third parties and members of the public for some of their practice sessions. Remember to get them all to sign confidentiality agreements if the exercise contains sensitive commercial information.

ACTION

Action involves calling the team together to consider a real or 'live' potential crisis. The first job may be to decide whether the situation merits being declared as a crisis. This does not, obviously, apply to the sudden emergency, but some 'simmering' issues can be difficult to gauge. Some companies have come to rue the day when they have put a full-blown crisis plan into action only to find that it has exacerbated the problem rather than limited its damage.

FOLLOW-UP

Follow-up is crucial for several reasons. It is only by analysing the results of a crisis-handling situation that you find out what worked and what did not. The crisis team will also be needed to coordinate the various internal and external enquiries that are sure to follow an event worthy of calling the team into action in the first place.

See Appendix 1 for a typical agenda for a crisis team's first meeting after an incident.

A CONCLUDING NOTE

Some crisis experts have recommended, and we agree, that it is sometimes necessary to be imaginative when, as chairperson, you are selecting your crisis team. Part of your formula for a successful group will be to have the correct mixture of personalities and temperaments. In an ideal world you should include the logical thinker, the imaginative 'loads of ideas, not all of them practical' character, the natural communicator, the 'worst-case scenario' merchant, the pedant and, finally, the humorist. Personalities who should not be included are dramatists, those of a nervous disposition, slow decision-makers, nine-to-fivers and 'jobsworths'.

LEARNING POINTS

- Set up a crisis team that represents the key sections of the company or organization.
- Designate a deputy for each team member.
- Break down each team member's role into: preparation, implementation, practice, action and follow-up.
- Try to get a balance of personalities on the team.

15 Crisis planning and whistle-blowing

Remember that the first rule of crisis management is to get ahead of the situation and remain in charge of it throughout. This requires the identification of areas of vulnerability as the starting point. It is only by inspecting the status quo that it is possible to get a picture of where you are most likely to have problems.

In our experience, it is those companies that have taken the trouble to gain accreditation to one or more of the systems of business standards (ISO, BS and Investors in People) that have a clear advantage. The demands of these systems in terms of recording and cataloguing things about the business make it easier to check where a crisis might hit hardest.

'What if?' may be the question but it needs to be set against a checklist of potential hazards (see Figure 15.1).

WHAT IF THINGS GO WRONG IN
- Human resources?
- Finance?
- Engineering?
- Transport?
- Information technology?
- Telecommunications?
- Security?
- Customer relations?
- Corporate affairs?
- Business development?
- Research?
- Marketing?
- Sales?
- Training?
- Legal?

Figure 15.1 Potential hazards checklist

> *WHAT WOULD THE HUMAN RESOURCES DEPARTMENT DO IF THE COMPANY...*
> - experienced a fire/explosion/terrorist threat/kidnapping?
> - had a major IT failure?
> - had an ex-employee threatening legal action or exposure?
> - experienced a significant failure in recruiting suitable staff?
> - experienced a breakdown in health and safety procedures?
> - relocated?
> - made redundancies?
> - suffered significant major loss of key personnel (a regular problem in financial institutions)?

Figure 15.2 Example section of an impact-minimizing checklist

Representatives from each department of the business should then be asked to advise on the areas of vulnerability. Having done that, they need to quantify the impact on the business as a whole if something happened to exploit that area of susceptibility. This brings us to the actions that need to be put into place to minimize the impact (see Figure 15.2).

The list is not complete and the categories will vary from company to company but the procedure must be followed and regularly updated. In our experience, the people in these key departments will not only relish the opportunity to think the worst but will also be quite lurid in their descriptions of the consequences of things going wrong. When we run courses in crisis management and take with us what we regard as horrible scenarios we are often beaten in intensity by the employees themselves. It is they, after all, who know the potential for disaster and who will paint the picture in horrifying detail.

It is no good going through this exercise if the results are literally or metaphorically put on the shelf and never seen again. The subject must be regularly addressed in all staff communications (internal publications, e-mails, bulletin boards, Intranet) and it should be a fixed feature of any staff appraisals. Members of any organization should be encouraged to be not only self-critical but also to pass on information if they think that their department or the company as a whole may be in danger. Human resource people should be trained to embrace the whistle-blower (anonymously, if necessary) and not regard them as a 'pain in the neck'. Unfortunately, too many companies are tempted to blame the messenger rather than tackle the fundamental issues, and this can lead to frightening results (see case study 15.1).

CASE STUDY 15.1
British Biotech

In 1995 a company in Oxford, specializing in pharmaceuticals based on biotechnological research, became a publicly quoted company with shares offered at 50 pence each.

British Biotech, founded by Keith McCullagh, was eager to talk up the prospects of its principal drugs under research including Marimastat for cancer and Zacutex for pancreatitis. Throughout 1995 and 1996 news releases were sent to the media extolling the virtues of the new products and suggesting that the trials were going well.

Behind the scenes, however, a nasty piece of office politics was developing between the scientists and the company managers. The 45-year-old director of clinical research, Dr Andrew Millar, for example, was anxious about the results of the trials and the escalating costs – in particular, the directors' salaries which, in some cases, were as high as £250 000 per year.

He began lobbying the non-executive board members to get the general management to ease up on the claims that were being made for the drug tests and to put a ceiling on directors' pay of £100 000. He briefed shareholders on what he thought might be dangerous consequences for patients if the tests continued.

When Dr Millar felt that he had exhausted the 'behind the scenes' route, he decided to go public. The company, whose shares were now well over 300 pence each, was furious; it sent him home and prepared a legal case against him for disclosing commercially sensitive information. Company news releases spoke of him acting through pique because he had failed to get a board-level job and branded him as 'ill-informed' and 'irresponsible'. Dr Millar, an Oxford graduate who had worked on biotechnology projects all over the world, countersued for libel and wrongful dismissal.

A year later, the company dropped the charges and issued a statement saying that Dr Millar had always acted according to his professional ethics. His pay-off was reportedly £500 000 and it was also announced that the company founder, Keith McCullagh, was leaving. At various intervals the company also lost its chairman, commercial director, a medical director, a non-executive director and even the clinical director who had been brought in to take over from Dr Millar.

Adding to the mess was an accountant's report disclosing that Mr McCullagh and two directors had sold substantial numbers of their own shares just weeks before disclosing that one of the clinical trials had, indeed, been a failure.

As a result, the company's share price dropped to 15 pence, 42 staff were made redundant, the stock exchange announced an insider trading investigation and the US Securities and Exchange Commission issued a rare formal warning about the use of misleading news releases. This, in itself, was an embarrassment to the firm's public relations company which, in the normal run of things, should have been briefed on the true position and resigned if the company insisted on putting inaccurate information into the public domain.

A select committee of the House of Commons also held hearings into what had gone wrong.

The upshot was that a company that once came close to the Financial Times 100 Index became a small player with a totally restructured management. The whistle-blower, Dr Millar, could not find a new job and this prompted legislation in the UK to protect people who speak out in the public good.

The Financial Times probably summed it up best under the headline 'British Biotech becomes a victim of its own hype'. The article made the point that it was tempting for science-based companies to feed potential and existing shareholders with positive news no matter what the reality. It further pointed out that the scandal had hit the credibility of the whole sector by a factor of many millions of pounds.

What are the crisis management lessons to be learnt?

This was clearly a 'simmering' dispute which got totally out of hand, but which could have been dealt with at a much earlier stage and out of the glare of publicity. Once it did become public, the company seems to have panicked and put out totally misleading information. Dr Millar was forced to protect his reputation by suing and, when the company dropped the case, it was made to look completely incompetent.

Perhaps the worst thing of all is that, even after the initial disaster, the company learned no crisis management lessons. It continued to invite journalists to the research headquarters and talked up the trial results. In one case, a writer from the *Daily Telegraph* was persuaded that all was going well just six weeks before the company announced yet another research failure.

Directors on the board, who knew that their actions were now in the full media spotlight, decided to trade in their own shares. While they did not break any laws, the public perception of their action was that it was unsavoury to say the least.

CRISIS PLANNING AND WHISTLE-BLOWING

> The strange thing is that this crisis management disaster was not perpetrated by an old-fashioned company that was set in its ways. It was a thoroughly modern and fast-thinking operation, presumably dazzled by its own brilliance and blind to the warnings of at least one expert.

Some organizations have successfully got around the 'whistle-blower problem' with a system based on anonymity. The RAF, for example, was worried that pilots would not necessarily report procedural errors or close shaves in case these counted against them on their personnel evaluations. The answer was to put a box in the crew rooms so that the aircrew could notify things that had gone wrong anonymously. There is no reason why other organizations shouldn't adopt this idea as part of any early warning system for a crisis.

All warnings should be passed to a crisis coordinator whose job it is to consult on whether it is serious enough to call a meeting of the crisis team (see Chapter 14). It is very important to make this judgement correctly since there is nothing worse than declaring a crisis and involving other people when it is no such thing. That may, in itself, trigger unwarranted rumours and speculation. Even if the crisis team is not needed, the coordinator must make it a matter of priority to minute exactly what has occurred and justify their actions.

If the crisis team is called to arms, it must establish clear lines of communication both internally and externally. Who should be told and by what method? Who is going to cascade the information and to whom? Will it be open (for others to see)? Or discreet? However, bear in mind that, in these days of voice- and e-mail, nothing is quite as safe as it was when vital information was carried by horseback around the country in an envelope with a wax seal!

A similar exercise needs to be undertaken for external audiences and, in this case, the security of the information must be absolute. It should, however, be part of the exercise to ask 'What happens if this information leaks?'.

Throughout this preparation period it is crucial to ask yourself and your team what is the worst that can happen. You can always work backwards from that but hardly ever forwards when things have gone pear-shaped and are out of control. Do not ever accept the word of anyone in the organization who says 'It can never happen'. Bitter experience tells us that, if it can happen, it will. Chief executives often call us in to prepare them for important meetings with investors, analysts, select committees and so on. We will give them the worst possible ride only to receive a letter of appreciation a few days later, saying 'It was nothing like as rough as it was with you lot.'

Watch out for those in your organization who like to keep information hidden. Fiefdoms are all very well, but can leave you exposed to danger if they are allowed to keep damaging information to themselves.

If you have access to what they have at least you can put in place damage limitation procedures such as background information documents and statements that can be sprung into action immediately. The media and other outside audiences will be easier to influence if you appear to be open and honest. The most natural reaction in a crisis is to wait until everything has been sorted out before communicating properly. In fact, the opposite tactic is the best option, although you must never disseminate information that has only been half-digested.

LEARNING POINTS

- Get ahead of the situation and stay there.
- Explore all areas of vulnerability.
- Put in place damage limitation procedures.
- Agree all internal and external communications systems.
- Establish early warning machinery.
- Do not declare a crisis unnecessarily.
- Always practise worst-case scenarios.
- Prepare background information for instant release.

Part III

Appendices

Appendix 1: The crisis team and crisis centre

CHECKLIST OF DUTIES FOR CRISIS TEAM MEMBERS

CHAIRPERSON

Who should be on the team?

What character types?

What roles should I assign to each?

Who should deputize for each?

How many meetings per year?

How will I report to the board?

DEPUTY CHAIRPERSON

Am I being copied in on everything in case the chairperson is absent?

How am I going to communicate with the crisis team and how often?

Who is going to collate the crisis plan for me to activate?

How practical is the assignment of roles during an emergency?

What resources may be necessary?

How will I prepare and implement a special budget?

What process is in place to identify all suppliers and customers quickly?

HUMAN RESOURCES

What staff would be required in a worst-case scenario?

Have I got an easy-to-update staff list and contact numbers?

What are the training requirements?

Is there an easy-to-plot shift system and overtime arrangements in an emergency?

Are union contacts up-to-date?

Do we have back-up arrangements for additional supplies and equipment?

FINANCE

Do we have a contingency budget for emergencies?

How would it be activated?

Have we credit facilities in the event of a sudden crisis?

Do we have a fast-track system for spending money in a crisis?

Will I be able to gauge the financial impact of an emergency?

What mechanism have I got in place to speak swiftly to shareholders and analysts?

Have we purchased special insurance cover?

Do the banks know?

LEGAL AND INSURANCE

Have I copies of all key legal documents and insurance policies for safekeeping in the crisis room?

Do I have easy access and an out-of-hours contact list for all insurers, risk assessors and law firms?

Can I call on additional legal advice at short notice?

Have I a method of quickly assessing insurance and legal risks?

Can I quickly establish contact with Communications to discuss and approve news releases?

COMMUNICATIONS

Have I prepared an easy-to-understand background document on who we are, what we do and how we do it?

Is there a good stock of annual reports available?

Am I trained and prepared to be media spokesperson?

Have I drafted specimen news releases?

How will I deal with media inquiries?

Can I call on additional help?

How will I monitor what the media says?

Who are the key internal and external audiences?

What might our key messages be?

Have we retained a call centre to handle telephone enquiries?

OPERATIONS

Who will be in our crisis response team?

Can I call on additional technical support?

What outside contractors should be briefed on the crisis plan?

Have we a recovery programme and how does it work?

Have I got instant access to a budget for additional equipment and other materials?

HEALTH, SAFETY AND ENVIRONMENT

Have I easy access to mandatory regulations and notifications?

Do I have all out-of-hours contact numbers for environmental agencies?

Have I an easy-to-access list of local interest and community groups?

Do I have out-of-hours contacts for trade associations and other relevant companies?

Have we key contact numbers for internal and external medical support?

APPENDICES

RECORD-KEEPER

Have I a sample agenda if something sudden happens and we convene the crisis team?

How will I contact the team?

How will the paperwork and e-mails flow?

What must I record and how?

Do we have sufficient PA, secretarial, security, receptionist, telephone back-up, and are they trained?

TYPICAL AGENDA FOR A CRISIS TEAM'S FIRST MEETING AFTER AN INCIDENT

Has all the team been notified and the necessary emergency calls made?

Report on the incident from the Operations member or crisis coordinator.

What extra resources are needed, if any?

Damage report from the emergency service's incident commander, if applicable.

Human resources report.

Is there any media interest and what communications are needed?

Are statements and news releases ready for use?

Selection of spokesperson [*if not already done – this may depend on the nature of the crisis*].

Client/supplier situation report.

Identify needs:

- Accommodation
- Transport
- Personnel
- Utilities
- IT/Telecoms
- Technical taskforce.

Insurance and legal report.

Time/date/venue of next meeting.

CHECKLIST FOR CRISIS CENTRE

Have we selected a room big enough for the crisis team to operate over time?

Is there a separate room to think?

Have charts, maps, diagrams, contracts, staff lists, customer lists, client lists all been copied to a secure area of the room?

Do we have enough dedicated telephones and faxes for outbound calls only?

How many networked PCs do we need?

Have we telephones, radios, flipcharts and an ability to teleconference?

Are several numbered issues of the crisis plan in the room and regularly updated?

Are there facilities for drinks and snacks?

Are there easy-to-read plans of emergency assembly points, safety equipment and so on?

Have we a spare stock of mobile phones and pagers with rechargers?

Is there a good stock of stationery, background papers, draft news releases and annual reports?

Appendix 2: The spokesperson

CHECKLIST OF DUTIES

Has the database been updated with all internal and external contacts?

Are draft news releases ready?

Have we prepared easy-to-read background statements?

Are videos and photographs and biographies up-to-date?

Is there a list of potential third-party endorsees in existence?

Is the media centre fully equipped?

- TV
- Radio
- Video playback
- PCs
- Mobiles
- Quiet area
- Extra telephones
- Copier and printer
- Fax machine
- Stationery
- Annual reports
- Maps/diagrams

Have we organized monitoring of the media?

Are PR consultants organized?

Have we a database of journalists who write about us?

APPENDICES

KEY ADVICE FOR SPOKESPEOPLE

- Always be open, honest and accessible.
- Always return media calls.
- Fill communications vacuums.
- Do not speculate or answer hypothetical questions.
- Always participate in training sessions.
- Correct all inaccuracies or distortions.
- Be flexible.
- Show empathy and compassion.
- Be proactive not reactive.
- Remember that there is no such thing as 'off the record'.
- Never respond to a question with 'No comment'. It means 'guilty as charged'.
- Make sure that the communications team always appears to be part of management and 'in the loop'.
- Taperecord all interviews, if possible.
- Record all requests for information or interviews.
- Always keep control.
- Take the attitude that you have information to share.
- Seize the agenda and do not lose it.
- Be the authoritative source of information.
- Rehearse all presentations and interviews.
- Draw up sample questions and answers for all to use.
- Illustrate all key messages with anecdotes and analogies.

CHECKLIST FOR NEWS CONFERENCES

Have we enough to say to warrant a conference?

Is the room big enough?

Is there a separate room for interviews?

Who are we inviting?

Who should be on the panel? (*Hopefully not more than three – housekeeper (usually the spokesperson), strategist (MD or chairperson), technician (finance director, marketing, operations, for example.*)

Are there sufficient background information packs available?

Set a time limit.

Make sure that the journalists identify themselves when asking questions.

Have charts been prepared to explain any complicated issues?

Have refreshments been organized?

Is the sound system effective and does it work?

Have name badges been issued?

Has someone been appointed to take note of questions and answers so that things can be followed up?

Spread questions around with an emphasis on specialists.

Make the answers clear and simple.

Do not appear harassed or angry.

Watch for tricky questions before the session starts and afterwards.

Announce the time and place of the next briefing.

ENQUIRY LOG

PUBLICATION:

Title:

Address:

Telephone:

Fax:

E-mail:

REPORTER/CORRESPONDENT

Title:

Telephone:

Fax:

E-mail:

APPENDICES

REQUEST

Outline of article/programme:

What is wanted?
- Interview:
- Background briefing:
- Media pack:
- Photographs:
- Video:
- Filming facilities:
- Other:

OTHER PEOPLE BEING INTERVIEWED

Name:

Position/organization:

Name:

Position/organization:

Name:

Position/organization:

DEADLINES

Interview:

Copy:

Photographs:

OFFICE USE

Designated actions and deadlines:

Appendix 3: Training

An agreed part of any crisis communications plan must include a budget for training. Who should be trained and in what?

- **Crisis team**. Crisis management communications workshops at regular intervals. Theory and practice preferably every year.
- **Operations team**. Theory and practice at least every year. For a team undertaking fire or rescue work this should be practised and coordinated with the emergency services at regular intervals.
- **Receptionists/telephonists**. An 'introduction to crisis communications' course as part of their induction. Other courses can be organized to simulate dealing with different 'audiences' in a crisis. These staff members are the frontline troops in an emergency and are often neglected when crisis plans are drawn up. In our experience, they are rarely consulted or included in the loop and they should be. Most receptionists/telephonists tell us that they dread to think what might happen in a sudden emergency.
- **Security personnel**. Training in dealing with emergencies and the media on induction. Practical training, if possible, against a realistic scenario. Again, these people are frontline troops and should know what to do.
- **Human resources**. Should be represented on the crisis team and fully briefed on crisis scenarios. They play a major role in the aftermath of a crisis – particularly if it involves redundancies, death or injury.
- **IT/telecoms**. Should be represented on the crisis team. There are specialist courses run by sector experts on what to do in a high-tech crisis. Key personnel should be trained in the latest techniques.

Appendix 4: Media handling

PREPARATION CHECKLIST

Do I have the following in place?

Some easy-to-read background notes on the company or organization.

Supplies of annual reports ready to distribute.

Biographies for each key executive, along with still photographs.

A library of still pictures of each company building or operation.

Press packs.

Video footage of operations.

A media log to record inquiries (see Example A4.1).

Outgoing telephone lines to return media calls.

Enough staff media trained.

Enough spokespeople trained.

Media monitoring system in place.

Public relations consultancy in place for back-up.

Spare computer hardware and software.

Videoplayer, television and radio.

Photocopier.

Maps and diagrams of operations.

Bed, washing facilities and basic food and drink preparation.

APPENDICES

Spare mobile phones.

Teleconferencing equipment (if appropriate).

EXAMPLE A4.1
Media log

Journalist's name:

Job description:

Publication:

Address:

Telephone:

Fax:

E-mail:

Time and date of call:

Nature of call:

What is required:

    Background information:

    Interview:

    Photograph:

Deadline:

Internal contact:

Action:

Follow up:

Logged for the record:

Attach resulting article or transcript:

Appendix 5: Complaints against the media

COMPLAINTS AGAINST NEWSPAPERS AND MAGAZINES

Very often, a crisis can be precipitated by media coverage itself and, for emergency planning purposes, it is worth knowing how to complain about the coverage you receive.

The most important thing to remember is that, for historical reasons, the print media is unregulated except by the laws of libel and slander, whereas broadcasters are heavily regulated by parliament and other bodies. This makes a distinct difference to the rights you have as an individual or as representatives of a company or organization.

Newspaper editors pretend to take the complaints apparatus seriously because they have been pressured by politicians and other members of the 'establishment' whose postbags are sometimes overflowing with complaints about press behaviour. Occasionally, publications are forced to correct an error, publish an apology or retract allegations, but this is a rare occurrence and often takes place long after the damage has been done.

To be fair to some sections of the press, there are a number of publications that have set up their own complaints departments where an independent ombudsman is charged with investigating whether or not a complaint is justified. They can interview editorial staff, examine notebooks and look at evidence before giving a judgement in the publication involved. Their remit can even run to complaints about the use of language, political bias and offensive photographs.

The important thing, in a crisis, is to monitor what is being said in the press and complain when necessary – and as soon as possible. If you don't, the damaging, inaccurate or misleading information about you will be there for ever more. Furthermore, it will be resurrected every time another journalist is given the task of writing about you.

Like the freedom of information legislation that is often advocated, action to curb the activities of the press is easier talked about than enacted. Editors and

APPENDICES

journalists suspect that if Acts of Parliament were created, it would be the rich, the powerful and the criminal who would make use of the provisions to protect their activities. They would, in effect, use the legislation as a 'gagging order' against press reporting in the national interest. The late publisher, Robert Maxwell, is often cited in this context. He regularly threatened injunctions and other legal devices to intimidate the press into holding back on publishing information they had about him.

In reality, the poor, the vulnerable and those genuinely aggrieved by press coverage, currently stand little chance of redress. Our advice to everyone on this is really quite simple: apply as much pressure as you can to correct wrong impressions or inaccuracies, but think long and hard before taking legal action. Lawsuits drag on because the court system moves very slowly and lawyers like to take as much valuable (to them) time as possible in preparations. A court hearing can also have the effect of highlighting the damaging information rather than extracting damages. It can also be counterproductive in other ways since the opposition may be allowed to include, in their evidence, potentially damaging information about you that played no part in the original article.

In other words, a court hearing can turn into a trial of you rather than them. History is littered with cases that have broken rich and powerful organizations which thought that they could face down the press.

Always remember that newspaper and magazine publishers are usually insured against court actions and they generally take the view that the world is littered with people who think they can try it on to add wealth to their pension fund.

COMPLAINTS AGAINST BROADCASTERS

When it comes to broadcasting, the situation is significantly different because the industry is regulated by Acts of Parliament. These Acts have been toughened over the years at the instigation of parliamentarians and civil servants.

Independent television and radio are covered by the Broadcasting Act while the BBC is covered by something known as the 'Charter' which comes up for renewal at regular intervals. The BBC's senior management spends half its working lives worrying about 'renewing the Charter'.

All this means that government and parliament have significant power over broadcasting activities that they do not have over the press. As a result, the broadcasters have created guidelines to educate their staff on their obligations under the regulations that govern them. These are weighty documents that

COMPLAINTS AGAINST THE MEDIA

cover all aspects of broadcasting from drama to religion, and transmission masts to taste.

What is of most interest to those of us charged with dealing with a crisis are those chapters that lay down obligations on editors, producers, researchers and correspondents when they are working on a broadcast that requires the cooperation of a company, organization or individual. Without going into too much technical detail, the producer guidelines say, quite clearly, that there must be a 'doctrine of fairness' when you approach people to cooperate in a news, current affairs or documentary item.

If the subject of the programme wants certain information what the broadcaster is up to, they are entitled to an open, fair and frank explanation. The broadcaster is not allowed to mislead you about what the item or programme is about. The programme-makers must provide housekeeping information such as who the producers are, who the reporters will be, the date and time of the transmission and the likely audience. They should also provide, if asked, fundamental information about the approach being taken, who else is likely to be interviewed and what other information may be required to help you make your mind up whether or not to participate.

If a company has completed this procedure but decides not to take part in the production itself and the programme turns out to be damaging, it has the right to report the programme to the Broadcasting Standards Commission. This is a body with substantial powers to force broadcasters to transmit detailed apologies and adjudications at the exact time the original programme was broadcast.

The important thing to remember here is that the Commission will only hear a case if you supply the details, in writing, of how you were misled.

The key word here is 'participate'. The act of asking for detailed information about the programme constitutes participation regardless of whether or not you actually put someone up for interview.

The crisis tip is to make sure that all broadcasting requests are accompanied by detailed faxes or e-mails. These are timed documents that can be used to keep the broadcasters feet to the fire.

Beware, however, of the grey area in all this – that is, the type of programme described as 'investigative', 'consumer' or 'watchdog'. Some of these are legitimate news and current affairs programmes and have the same obligations under the producer guidelines. Others fall into the 'entertainment' or 'showbusiness' category, and no one seems to know whether the guidelines apply. This is one reason why, a few years ago, several major companies pooled their resources to complain about the activities of the BBC1 programme *Watchdog* which, they claimed, was being unfair in its journalism. No direct action was taken as a result, but it acted as a well-publicized 'shot across the bows'.

APPENDICES

Our general advice is to participate in broadcast programmes if you possibly can because, no matter how hostile the presentation of allegations, if you have a reasonable case it will be aired. However, if there is absolutely no advantage in appearing, then refuse to do so. You can always issue a statement covering your side of the case, but remember that it will almost certainly be given to a professional actor who will almost certainly inject a sarcastic or sneering tone to their voice for additional effect!

COMPLAINTS AUTHORITIES

Listed below are the main bodies that deal with media complaints:

Press Complaints Commission
1 Salisbury Square
London EC4Y 8JB
Tel: 0207 353 1248
Helpline: 0207 353 3732

This is a self-regulatory body overseen by key editors from various parts of the publishing sector. Adjudications are made, but the Commission has no regulatory powers to enforce its decisions.

Press Council
5–7 Vernon Yard
London W11 2DX
Tel: 0207 792 9400
Fax: 0207 243 2263
E-mail: info@presscouncil.com

Broadcasting Standards Commission
7 The Sanctuary
London SW1P 3JS
Tel: 0207 233 0544
Fax: 0207 233 0397
E-mail: bsc@bsc.org.uk

The Commission considers complaints about violence, sex and matters of taste and decency from any listener or viewer about radio and television programmes. It also investigates allegations of unjust or unfair treatment or infringement of privacy from those with a direct interest in the programme.

It has the power to force a television or radio programme to broadcast an adjudication made again them.

The Independent Television Commission
33 Foley Street
London W1W 7TL
Tel: 0207 255 3000
Fax: 0207 405 7062
E-mail: publicaffairs@itc.org.uk

This Commission handles complaints about programmes and advertisements on ITV, Channels 4 and 5, satellite and cable services.

The Radio Authority
Holbrook House
14 Great Queen Street
London WC2B 5DG
Tel: 0207 430 2724
Fax: 0207 405 7062
E-mail: reception@radioauthority.org.uk

This body handles similar complaints about independent radio programmes.

British Broadcasting Corporation
Programme Complaints Unit
PO Box 1922
Glasgow G2 3WT
Tel: 08780 100222
Fax: 0141 307 5770
E-mail: info@bbc.co.uk

Note: Remember, too, that several of the national newspapers have ombudsmen who deal with complaints from readers. They will often publish corrections or apologies if they find that they were in the wrong. They also have the role of explaining the publication's policy on reporting certain events or issues that have a bearing on the stance being taken in their editorial columns.

Appendix 6: Information technology

The computerization and installation of other information technology in recent years has created a new category of crisis that needs the special attention of a crisis team. The checklist below covers factors that need addressing with the help of the IT specialist on the team. Note that this list is not exhaustive because the technology is changing and moving all the time.

INFORMATION TECHNOLOGY CHECKLIST

Have we enough security (firewalls and so on)?

How often do we change or amend passwords?

Have we a complete and reliable back-up system?

What do we do to check for hackers?

Do we sufficiently restrict access?

Can we spot the creation of false accounts?

Can we spot false credits, cheques, goods or invoices?

Do we provide information about our hardware or software?

If so, how do we know what the information is used for?

Do we monitor the costs of calls/Internet access? (*A higher call rate is usually an indication of hacking or misuse.*)

Can we spot-check e-mail traffic?

Is there too much sensitive information on our bulletin boards?

APPENDICES

Can we check for the misuse of the Internet?

Do we monitor employees' use of company mobile phones?

Asking the questions in this form, and analysing the answers, will provide a valuable template for the areas in which the organization may be vulnerable. It is also worth asking outside specialist firms to audit the IT situation in the same way that you use outside auditors or legal experts to look over the accounts and contracts.

Appendix 7: Crisis and the World Wide Web

The existence and development of the Web over recent years has added an altogether new dimension to crisis planning – some of it beneficial, some not. The fact that, on the Web, people can say what they like about you and your organization can act as a good early warning system about a 'simmering' crisis. It can also spread untrue rumour and gossip that can be damaging if it is not dealt with swiftly.

One international lobbying group, PETA (People for the Ethical Treatment of Animals) claims to have had a major success in their Internet campaign against the McDonalds hamburger company. They regularly criticized the company under compelling headlines such as 'Cruelty to Go', 'Animals Deserve a Break Today' and 'Son of Ron: America's No 1 Serial Killer'.

Monitoring what is said about you on the Internet is vital in any crisis planning exercise. If you have your own website, it needs to be watched for anyone criticizing your operation and it must be regularly updated with information you are putting into the public domain including news releases, statements, annual reports and advertising and marketing campaigns. Inaccuracies and misleading statements must be corrected immediately. Chatrooms should also be monitored and, if there is a debate about you or your activities, join in. Put things right and be seen to be engaged. If you don't, damaging material will stay on the public record.

It is not enough just to participate, however. If there is valid criticism that can be corrected, then do so and tell Web users how you have put things right. Using the Web is the equivalent of 'chatting over the garden fence' except that most of the latter type of conversations do not make it into the media. A scandal instigated through the Web can be picked up by journalists in an instant. The Web can be particularly damaging in this respect, because it is largely unregulated and is not covered under the laws of libel. Anyone can say almost anything they like about you, and there is no redress except instant rebuttal.

Some companies and organizations have built in so-called 'dark sites' on the Internet that are only accessible to their crisis managers. These give them

APPENDICES

access to position papers held in reserve, standby news releases, and online databases of journalists and other opinion-formers.

The most important thing to remember about interaction with the Web is to make sure that your Web-based corporate messages exactly replicate those being given to external audiences using more conventional corporate affairs methods.

INTERNET CHECKLIST

Do we have an easy-to-access website and is it monitored regularly?

Are public statements, releases and reports put on the website and regularly updated?

Is the site vulnerable to hackers?

If there is criticism on the site itself or others, what is our procedure for rebutting what is said?

If the criticism or reporting is true, what are we going to do about it?

Should we set up 'dark sites' for use in a crisis and, if so, will they be secure?

Appendix 8: County Major Civil Emergency Plan

We have taken our typical County Emergency Plan from our home county of Hampshire. This is a part of the country that is heavily residential in places with several major towns and cities. The county also has a number of military establishments (both obvious and secret), and a high number of potential terrorist targets and hazardous process industries. In addition, it has a number of airports and coastal installations.

COUNTY AND DISTRICTS MAJOR CIVIL AND EMERGENCY PLAN 1999

HAMPSHIRE CONSTABULARY

Hampshire is divided into three mainland divisions further divided into 18 territorial sub-divisions. The Isle of Wight is an additional territorial sub-division. Whatever the legal and professional responsibilities of other parties and organisations, who play a crucial part in the management of a major disaster or civil emergency, control and co-ordination is simply a necessary pre-condition to enable the other emergency services' inputs to be brought into effect. Unless there is a single control at some level there will be competing and confusing interests.

The primary areas of police responsibility may be summarised as follows:

1. The saving of life in conjunction with other Emergency Services.
2. Co-ordination of the Emergency Services and other subsidiary organisations.
3. The protection and preservation of the scene.
4. The investigation of the incident. Whether a crime has been committed or not, in conjunction with other investigative bodies where applicable.
5. The collection and dissemination of casualty information.
6. The identification of victims on behalf of the coroner.
7. Notification to relatives.
8. Press and media liaison.
9. Restoration of normality at the earliest opportunity.

APPENDICES

HAMPSHIRE FIRE AND RESCUE SERVICE

1. Mobilise and dispatch five appliances and manpower to the scene of the accident.
2. Implement any pre-determined arrangements relating to the location and nature of the incident.
3. Undertake fire fighting and rescue operations. (At fires and incidents with a risk of fire, the senior fire officer has a statutory duty to be in charge of fire fighting and its associated functions.)
4. Carry out certain salvage operations where considered necessary to protect goods and property.
5. Establish a Fire Service Control point at the scene of the incident and forward controls.
6. Establish liaison with Police and Ambulance Control.
7. Provide cutting gear, rescue equipment, winches and emergency lighting for rescue operations.
8. Assist the medical services in access to trapped casualties.
9. Arrange and provide firemen to be available with protective clothing and breathing apparatus.
10. Determine unsafe areas and advise on the need for evacuation and inform Police Incident Commander of serious hazards or contamination.
11. Provide equipment and personnel for the implementation of decontamination procedures for persons involved.
12. Perform first aid actions as advised by Service Fire Control and on-site specialists with regard to spillages etc., involving materials and assist disposal authorities as required.
13. Implement mutual aid arrangements with neighbouring Fire Services as appropriate.
14. Provide communications sets for incident ground communications.
15. Contact, through Service Control, local or national firms for the supply of pre-arranged specialist equipment and for the Home Office Supply and Transport Stores for the loan of emergency Fire Service appliances and equipment, as appropriate.
16. Provide assistance and manpower and other services as requested subject to availability.

AMBULANCE SERVICE

1. Receive emergency calls from the Emergency Services and other sources.
2. Despatch ambulances to the scene of the emergency.
3. Alert the geographically appropriate listed hospitals of the possibility of a major emergency.
4. Receive, from the first ambulance at the scene, confirmation of the nature of the emergency.
5. Stand down the alerted hospitals OR
6. Confirm a major emergency situation exists with nomination of the designated and any supporting hospitals.
7. Confirm designated and any supporting hospitals to the police.

8. Confirm to the designated hospitals any requirement for a Site Medical Officer and Mobile Medical Teams and arrange the provision of ambulance vehicles for their transportation to the scene.
9. Provide a senior ambulance officer at the scene of the emergency to act as 'Ambulance Incident Officer'.
10. Liaise at the scene with the Police (or Fire Brigade) who will be co-ordinating on-site activity.
11. Despatch to the scene of the emergency ambulances, emergency stores vehicles and, as appropriate, a Mobile Ambulance Control, the latter to be co-located with the controls of the other services.
12. Call for assistance in the provision of ambulances, where necessary, from the British Red Cross and St John Ambulance.
13. Provide identifying accoutrements for the Medical Incident Officer.
14. Establish radio communications from the scene of the emergency to the designated hospitals and if required radio communication with any officers deployed to designated Local Authority Emergency Centres.
15. Forward to the designated and supporting hospitals any information acquired at the scene relating to toxic or radiation hazards and possible contamination of casualties.
16. Determine at the scene the evacuation priorities for casualties and the hospitals to which they are to be sent as necessary, spreading the casualty load by using supporting hospitals for the minor injury category.
17. Advise the activated hospital on the prevailing situation and the categories and estimated times of arrival of casualties.
18. Organise further ambulance cover for the routine tasks by redeploying resources between ambulance stations or by appropriate arrangements with other ambulance services like St John and BRC.
19. Provide an Ambulance Liaison Officer at the designated hospitals to supervise the unloading and turn-round of ambulances.
20. Organise the relief of ambulance crews in the event of a prolonged emergency.
21. Confirm to the designated and supporting hospitals when there are no further casualties at the scene and that stand-down arrangements can be implemented.
22. Organise transportation for patients who may be discharged or transferred from the designated hospitals.
23. Provide ambulances or organise helicopter evacuation of casualties from the designated hospitals to specialist centres.
24. Take out of service any ambulances and crews that may have been exposed to contamination and to organise appropriate decontamination with the Fire Service.

HEALTH AUTHORITY/PUBLIC HEALTH

In any emergency where public health issues may be a factor, particularly where there is significant pollution or where there are significant levels of casualties, the Public Health Department of the Local Health Authority should be alerted. In areas of public health other than the acute services offered by the Ambulance Service and receiving hospitals, the Consultant in Communicable Disease Control (CCDC) or deputy, based at the Health Authority, have responsibility for addressing the public health

APPENDICES

implications of emergency situations. They will be able to advise on most aspects of public health particularly in cases of oil, chemical or other toxic pollution or where radiological, biological or bacteriological hazards may be present.

In relevant emergencies where a tactical command centre has been established, the CCDC will go to tactical command but a public health doctor will be available to give public health advice at a strategic level. Where there is no tactical command, it is likely that the CCDC will, in the first instance, go to the local District Authority Emergency Centre.

CITY, BOROUGH AND DISTRICT COUNCIL

1. Provide a point of contact to receive alerts and warnings.
2. Identify, set up and staff an Emergency Control Centre.
3. Arrange for a comprehensive communications system to be established.
4. Alert the appropriate District Council Departments, County Social Services and Education Departments and other authorities as appropriate.
5. Collect information, refine and assess requirements.
6. Send a liaison officer to the Police Incident Control.
7. Determine, provide and deploy available resources as appropriate.
8. Establish a system for disseminating Local Authority information to the public in the early stages usually in co-operation with the Police.
9. Alert and liaise, where appropriate, with Central Government Departments, other public bodies and organisations that may be involved in a crisis.
10. Liaise with the County Council for the supply of additional resources.
11. Arrange alternative or transit accommodation for the homeless if Rest Centres are unable to be used.
12. Assist in the provision of food and feeding facilities.
13. Arrange for the provision of emergency sanitation, clothing and other welfare items, where necessary in conjunction with other agencies.
14. Arrange for the re-housing of families as required.
15. Clear debris and restore roadways.
16. Arrange inspection and emergency repairs to properties and premises.
17. Implement environmental health measures.
18. Provide accommodation in Local Authority premises if requested by the Police for media handling or other services.
19. Maintain financial records of Local Authority expenditure and make arrangements for funding.
20. Provide a basis for deployment of volunteers from the public as appropriate.

COUNTY COUNCIL

1. Provide a point of contact to receive alerts and warnings.
2. Alert, if appropriate, District Authorities and County Council Departments.
3. Support District Authorities with County Council resources.
4. Arrange for external resources for use by the County and, where appropriate, District Authorities.
5. Set up and staff the County Emergency Centre and provide extra communication facilities, if required.

COUNTY MAJOR CIVIL EMERGENCY PLAN

6. Take overall responsibility for co-ordination and provide communications networks when more than one District is involved.
7. Alert and liaise, where appropriate, with Central Government Departments, other public bodies and any other organisation that may be involved with the crisis.
8. Maintain financial records of County Council expenditure and make arrangements for funding.
9. Exercise any authority that may be delegated by Central Government under certain circumstances.

COUNTY CHIEF EXECUTIVE

1. Ensure the proper management and direction of County activities.
2. Co-ordinate the activities of District Councils as appropriate.
3. Arrange for the alerting of the Emergency Committee as required.
4. Report to the Emergency Committee or elected members.
5. Arrange for the establishment of a decision making group.
6. Determine if and when the County Emergency Centre or an Operations Room is to be activated and who should attend from the decision making group.
7. Provide an officer for dealing with the media and provide arrangements for dealing with the media.
8. Provide a Management Information System to ensure information received is passed to the Management Team for decision making. Keep log of major events.
9. Make arrangements for the reception of Liaison Officers from outside agencies and provide services as required.

PROPERTY/BUSINESS/REGULATORY

PROPERTY

1. Establish an accommodation register for any emergency.
2. Provide factual knowledge on buildings and contact points for professional personnel with intimate knowledge of the buildings.
3. Draw on building contractors' resources.

ESTATES

1. Provide comprehensive details and plans of all land and buildings owned and occupied by the County Council.
2. Provide a wide range of professional property services and advice relating to either County Council properties or property in ownership/occupation of others that might be required at the time of a major civil emergency.

SCIENTIFIC SERVICES

1. Provide, if necessary, a Scientific Officer to join the decision making team.
2. Provide scientific advice centrally or at the scene.

APPENDICES

3. Provide identification and analytical facilities at the laboratory or incident.
4. Areas of expertise:

   Food contamination
   Water pollution
   Air pollution
   Land pollution
   Toxicity and risk assessment
   Health and safety
   Toxic and hazardous chemical

TRADING STANDARDS

1. Provide, if necessary, the Head of Regulatory Services to join the decision making team.
2. Provide an organisation, on behalf of the County, for the co-ordination of matters relating to the Food and Environmental Protection Act and the implementation of activities on behalf of the County.
3. Implement such Animal Health measures as are necessary including activities under the Rabies Contingency Plan and the Foot and Mouth contingency plan.
4. Establish the necessary liaison with other organisations and services in respect of the above matters.

SOCIAL SERVICES DEPARTMENT

1. HQ Social Services has the managing, co-ordinating and supporting responsibility when area staff request help.
2. Areas are responsible for managing, establishing and staff rest centres.
3. Liaise with the Education Department if schools or colleges are involved.
4. Liaise with the Housing Department/Housing Association/Major Private landlord when disaster affects individuals in that accommodation.
5. Arrange transport to get people to assembly points.
6. Establish, manage and staff rest centres with assistance of the WRVS and Red Cross.
7. Liaise with designated hospitals regarding the accelerated release of patients and the consequent need for domiciliary support.
8. Co-ordinate the psychological and social support required in a major emergency. The Social Services manager will activate the Major Incident Support Team through Team Co-ordinators. The team will provide support for survivors, their families and friends along with those involved in the rescue and anyone else affected by the emergency.

COUNTY SURVEYORS DEPARTMENT

1. Provide, where necessary, the County Surveyor or substitute to join the decision making group.
2. Resource the County Surveyors Emergency Control Centre.

3. Provide an organisation to mobilise contractors for road clearance, demolition and support for Emergency Services.
4. Provide an officer to attend the County Emergency Centre to co-ordinate use of transport resources as required.
5. Establish the necessary liaison with other organisations in these matters and advise on the use of the highway network.

COUNTY TREASURERS DEPARTMENT

1. To establish an appropriate financial organisation to ensure the maintenance of existing financial arrangements.
2. Speed the introduction of emergency arrangements.
3. Payments for emergency staff, equipment and supplies.
4. Liaise with other public authorities to ensure effective financial arrangements are in force.

EDUCATION DEPARTMENT

1. The department has a role to provide feeding officers and centres.
2. A Director of Education or substitute will join the decision making group at County headquarters.
3. Make education facilities premises available as required for accommodation for homeless people or for the use of Police and Social Services.
4. Make arrangements for provision of heating, lighting and sanitation services.
5. Make arrangements for food for emergency feeding.
6. Make arrangements for the distribution of emergency food and drink containers.
7. Make arrangements for staffing of school kitchens.

COUNTY SUPPLIES OFFICE

1. A County Supplies Officer to join the decision making group.
2. Designate staff for operation duties.
3. Establish contact points for provision of goods and services.
4. Liaise with other organisations and government departments.
5. Provide from stock items listed in the supplies department catalogue.
6. Provide transport and distribution service using fleet and service vans.
7. Make available delivery drivers with the necessary HGV licences.

WOMEN'S ROYAL VOLUNTARY SERVICE

1. Provide a point of contact for call-out.
2. Deploy members, equipment and stores in support of the Emergency Services and Local Authorities.
3. Assist in the care of homeless persons in rest centres.
4. Provide light refreshments and the provision of meals with members of the Emergency Services and Local Authorities.
5. Provide and issue second hand clothing.

APPENDICES

6. Provide welfare services in hospitals if required.
7. Provide those trained in 'victim support'.

BRITISH RED CROSS

1. Implement call-out system for members.
2. Support the Ambulance Service as required.
3. Supply qualified members to hospitals as required.
4. Help staff Emergency Centres.
5. Provide welfare support for victims and families.
6. Ensure that all members wear Red Cross identification.

ST JOHN AMBULANCE

1. Support Ambulance service and hospitals as required.
2. Support District Health Authority activities.
3. Set up and staff Emergency First Aid Centres.
4. Support 'after care services' as required.

THE CLERGY

1. Implement a Clergy Control.
2. Make arrangements to staff Local Authority Control Centre.
3. Attendance of Clergy Site Director.
4. To provide personnel for counselling and guidance to victims, relatives and anyone else who may be in distress.
5. To attend the injured and dying.
6. Attend mortuaries.
7. Comfort the bereaved.

CARING AGENCIES

1. Give support to the statutory agencies on a 24 hour basis and provide a befriending service to all those who are in distress at the scene of an emergency.
2. Give support when the initial shock is over and when requested to do so by the requesting/co-ordinating authority.

Appendix 9: Situations

In this appendix we identify categories of crisis events so that you have, in effect, an instant manual. Although, from research, we know that sudden events are mercifully rare they do provide management and staff with an instant opportunity to either shine or fail. A crisis is, if you like, a raw test of how the company is run. Prepreparation, following the guidelines outlined here, will be of considerable help.

We have broken up foreseeable events into the following groups:

- Accidents and disasters
- Other sudden threats to business
- Information technology failure
- Telecommunications failure.

ACCIDENTS AND DISASTERS

Accidents and disasters can be broadly defined as internal, external or in transit. Those that happen on your own premises are internal; those that affect other businesses but have an impact on you are external; and those that occur in transit are a little of both – particularly if they involve third parties such as transport contractors.

Internal and external accidents and disasters include:

- fire
- explosion
- flood
- hurricane
- pollution (incoming/outgoing)

APPENDICES

- breakage
- earthquake
- building collapse.

In-transit accidents and disasters include:

- road crash/spillage/breakage
- rail crash/spillage/breakage
- air crash/spillage/breakage
- water transport/crash/spillage/breakage
- postal/courier crash/spillage/breakage.

Note: If any of the above happens to you, your suppliers or clients it can justifiably be categorized by you as a crisis and should prompt consideration of calling together the crisis team.

CHECKLIST OF IMMEDIATE ACTIONS

Alert emergency services.

Direct staff to assembly points.

Alert all members of the crisis team.

Notify parent/sister companies.

Alert utilities:

- telecoms supplier
- water board
- gas supplier
- electricity supplier
- Highways Agency
- Health Protection Agency.

Call in PR consultancy.

Notify trade association.

Activiate back-up management.

Call in extra receptionists, telephonists and security personnel.

Note: A 999 emergency call will usually trigger the following notifications as a matter of course:

- fire service
- police service
- ambulance service/local hospital
- humanitarian back-up (the Salvation Army, social services, the Red Cross)
- the Weather Bureau
- the media.

CHECKLIST OF ACTIONS AFTER THE IMMEDIATE EMERGENCY IS OVER

Contact:

- regulators/planners
- Health and Safety Executive/Environment Agency
- customers
- suppliers
- union representatives
- local councillors
- local MP/MEP
- insurance assessors
- banks
- legal representatives
- property managers
- postal authorities
- landlord
- furniture/equipment suppliers.

Engage a company to run a hotline for ongoing enquiries.

Note: Many insurance companies issue their clients with computer disks to store the information required for the above actions to work as smoothly as possible. Names, addresses, telephone numbers and other vital information such as policy numbers, bank accounts and so on can be entered in advance and updated at regular intervals.

Members of the crisis team should have these disks with them at all times.

THE FOUR STAGES OF MEDIA COVERAGE

Arguably, one of the most experienced crisis management teams in the world, the London Metropolitan Police, take the view that how a disaster has been handled depends heavily on the amount of media coverage it attracts and how

APPENDICES

that unfolds. In their publication *Civil Emergencies and the Media* they list four definable stages of media coverage at an emergency or disaster:

- **Mayhem**. The immediate aftermath. Characterized by a mad scramble to know what, where, when, why and how it all happened and also by a need to get photographs.
- **Mastermind**. A search for all the relevant background information and history (see Example A9.1, 'The *Marchioness* disaster') below.
- **Manhunt**. The search for fault, error and the heads that must roll.
- **The epilogue**. The long-term aftermath and follow-up, the inquiries, trials, memorial services, recommendations, documentaries and the pressure groups.

The Metropolitan Police make the point that the first of these stages will manifest itself very quickly – within 24 hours. The epilogue, however, can last for years.

> **EXAMPLE A9.1**
> **The *Marchioness* disaster**
> The following questions were posed to the London Metropolitan Police in the aftermath of the *Marchioness* boat disaster on the Thames in London in 1989.
>
> - Who made the first emergency calls?
> - Which emergency services got there first?
> - How many rescuers and rescue vehicles were involved?
> - How had they heard and from whom?
> - How many times has this happened before?
> - What sort of training is provided on the river?
> - Can the media have facilities on the rescue boats?
> - How many passengers/dead/survivors?
> - When and where will the inquest be held?
> - Will the American victims' families be better off suing in the USA?
> - What are the statutory requirements/rights of way on the river, police powers to arrest under the Police and Criminal Evidence Act?
> - What are powers of the various regulatory authorities involved?
> - What is the history of pleasure craft on the river?
>
> And many more besides...
>
> Hundreds of media personnel and members of the public gathered on the river banks to watch the boat being raised. Survivors were interviewed, sometimes to the point of harassment.

> Unfounded rumours ran rife about a 'gay party' being on board and the risks of rescuers contracting AIDS and hepatitis. The media were particularly unhappy about being denied the best vantage point, Southwark Bridge, apparently for reasons of taste rather than for any operational reasons.
> *Source*: Taken from Metropolitan Police (1999).

OTHER SUDDEN THREATS TO BUSINESS

These types of threat are becoming more common all over the world, and all companies are recommended to include them in their crisis planning even if the prospect of them happening seems remote. In this category we would include:

- terrorism
- sabotage
- espionage
- violent crime
- civil unrest
- industrial action
- product tampering.

When faced with events of this nature, additional factors must be carefully considered before embarking on notifications.

In the case of terrorism, sabotage, espionage and violent crime, agencies of the state over and above the emergency services may become involved. The security services (both home and abroad) may have an interest in restricting information.

The armed services may have similar requirements for security. It is important to remember that, when the police and security services are involved, you may be forced to give up freedom of action. During terrorist or kidnapping situations, product-tampering or blackmail operations, they may ask the media to impose a 'news black-out'. This is done with the agreement of editors on the absolute condition that, when the immediate danger is over, all participants including the companies and organizations involved will give a full and comprehensive briefing as soon as possible. Their concern is that organizations facing an embarrassing, rather than dangerous, situation will try to enforce a black-out to save their own skins.

Civil unrest or industrial action may also involve the interests of politicians, senior civil servants, trade unions, the Home Office, the Welsh Assembly, the Scottish Office and Parliament or the Northern Ireland Office or Assembly.

APPENDICES

Product tampering and product recall could involve: advertising agencies buying space to warn the public; trade associations to speed information to other companies in a similar position; clients who have bought the product and who must now supervise the recall (for example, supermarkets, distributors, shops and clubs); government watchdog agencies; pressure groups; and consumer organizations.

A hotline may be needed immediately, and companies for which a product recall is a possibility should make arrangements for this in advance. The point at which a product is to be recalled is not the time to be interviewing companies that can provide you with a call centre manned 24 hours a day by people who need to be briefed on what they are talking about.

INFORMATION TECHNOLOGY FAILURE

Most companies and organizations are now so totally dependent on computer hardware and software that special arrangements need to be made under the crisis communications plan.

IT CHECKLIST

Have we backed up all our important data?

Is the data backed up and archived in a location distant from our own premises?

Are we insured to cover the cost of activating the back-up material?

Is all the material secured by the necessary firewalls to prevent unauthorized access or hacking?

Do we have sufficient consultant back-up if our own personnel are not available?

What arrangements are in place to make sure that off-site workers can link in with the network?

Are there credit facilities available to buy, lease or rent additional equipment?

TELECOMMUNICATIONS FAILURE

Companies and organizations who regularly rehearse their crisis communication systems usually report concerns about the overload created on their landline, mobile, radio and fax facilities. The following checklist helps to avoid congestion.

TELECOMMUNICATIONS CHECKLIST

Have we 'stand-alone' additional telecom facilities that can be used in an emergency – particularly for outbound calls?

Make sure that unwanted phone calls will not be taken through fax machines.

Are the batteries of radio telephones checked regularly?

Do we need to employ a company to take emergency calls in a crisis?

Have we an emergency roster of telephonists and receptionists?

Do they know how to categorize the calls and who to divert them to in an emergency?

Do the media have a special number and is it manned at all times?

Is there a teleconferencing system for intracompany links?

Does the crisis centre have dedicated faxes, phone lines and mobile phones?

REFERENCE

Metropolitan Police (1999), *Civil Emergencies and the Media*, rev. edn. Originally published February 1992.

Appendix 10: Crime

What research there has been into the sources of crises shows quite clearly that so-called 'white-collar' crime heads the league. It is this 'simmering' issue that requires special attention and eternal vigilance.

The universal truth is that if people inside or outside an organization see others using illegal methods and getting away with it, they may well be tempted to commit similar offences. A survey conducted by the Confederation of British Industry in 1999 indicated that 60 per cent of UK firms suffer from fraud each year at a cost of more than £12 billion. The management consultants, KPMG, estimate that incidents of fraud doubled between 1997 and 2000, with employee fraud showing the highest rate of growth.

INTERNAL CRIME

With internal crime it is especially important to try to anticipate at what point your internal resources will need to be boosted by outside experts and the police.

According to Michael Comer (1998), the following can, and should, be planned for:

- Theft
    - *Concealed*:
      Manipulation of records
      Manipulation of systems/personnel
    - *Unconcealed*:
      Smash-and-grab
      Warehouse theft
      Theft of deliveries
    - *Conversion*:
      Cheques/payments

APPENDICES

      False accounting credits
      Stolen goods
      Money-laundering
- Pilfering
- Diversion of cheques
- Fencing of cheques
- Fake or invented invoices
- Bribery
- Misrepresentation
- Company car fiddles
- Expenses scams
- Breaches of commercial confidentiality
- Breaches of computer security
- Drunkenness/drug-taking
- Vice
- Sexual/racial harassment
- Violence
- Top management fraud
- Payroll fraud
- Catastrophic fraud:
  - Bankruptcy
  - Loss of one year's profit or more
  - Collapse of share price
  - Forced change of ownership
  - Destruction of credibility
- Commission fiddles
- Forgery
- Inflation of hours worked
- Tampering with measuring equipment.

EXTERNAL CRIME

Michael Comer also identifies the following as external crime threats. Crisis communications planning must include procedures for detecting them:

PRICE-FIXING

Companies in industries that directly compete with each other are forbidden by international law to set identical prices. Trade enforcement agencies all over the world will take strong action against offenders and impose heavy fines.

The crisis team must make sure that internal systems are in place to spot price-fixing, particularly within the marketing departments. Staff should be trained to be aware of the dire consequences for the company if they are tempted to manipulate prices or create cartels within their markets.

The media are constantly on the alert for price-fixing in the retail sector, and companies that may be vulnerable to investigation should consider employing outside consultants to spot signs of trouble in this area.

PYRAMID SCHEMES

The most spectacular example of a corporate pyramid scheme was with the Enron Corporation in the United States. The organization became the biggest corporate bankruptcy in American history at the end of 2001 when it was revealed that it had established so-called 'partnerships' that were separate from the main corporate accounting system.

This was a new variation of what is known as a 'Ponzi' scheme which induces people to invest in unusually high-return ventures but where the money from new investors is used to pay out earlier ones. It is a basic fraud and, in its simplest form, amounts to what is known as a 'chain letter' where one person claims to have made considerable amounts of money from a scheme and encourages friends and acquaintances to invest when the project is doomed to failure.

Auditors and regulators should be on the look-out for these schemes. If they become known, they will trigger a crisis that must be dealt with as soon as possible.

FRAUD

Financial controllers and auditors must be instructed to look-out for assets that have gone missing. More importantly, they must watch out for signs that the perpetrator has concealed the loss by manipulating the books or misrepresenting transactions.

If fraud has been detected the crisis team must be informed as early as possible. The team must then decide whether the matter should be investigated and dealt with internally, or externally investigated by the police. It is a delicate issue and the temptation is often to try to deal with it 'in-house'. In our experience, however, if the details leak to the media or other outside audiences it is often better to have the third-party endorsement of the police whether or not their investigations lead to an actual prosecution.

APPENDICES

OVERCHARGING

Overcharging is usually done by parts of a company or organization that think they can get away with it because the customer will not notice. It is often done, too, by employees as part of a scheme to defraud their own management.

The difference between the accepted cost of goods and services and the amount actually charged can be 'creamed off' by corrupt employees with relative ease. Again, financial controllers and auditing teams must have systems to spot the practice and deal with it as a potential crisis. Regular senior management-level checks with customers about pricing should be commonplace.

As with so much to do with crisis work, it is essential to detect the practices early and act quickly as a deterrent to others.

PARALLEL TRADING

This is a hugely complex area of trade regulation, involving the bulk buying of, usually, branded goods in one country where the items are relatively cheap and transporting them to another where prices are high. The traders make their profit out of the price difference.

Although it is sometimes argued that this is fair practice since it is a healthy use of a free market, it can become an offence if the potential customers are misled into buying goods that are substandard or if import or tax controls have been circumvented.

Experts say that fraud is often involved in parallel trading, but there have also been some high-profile cases in which prosecutions have been brought as a matter of principle. For example, one UK supermarket chain started to buy branded jeans in other countries where they were cheaper so that it could sell them on at lower prices than their competitors and, as a result, were prosecuted by the manufacturers.

A crisis team should have legal advice to hand if their company is conducting parallel trading or such a practice is being used against it. Either way, the practice could seriously affect the company's trading position or its reputation for fair dealing.

COUNTERFEITING

Careful auditing and monitoring of sales is about the only recourse a company has if it suspects that its goods are being copied and sold as genuine. Many companies which sell branded goods and are most vulnerable to counterfeiting often employ ex-fraud squad officers or special investigators to find out where the fake goods are being manufactured and marketed. The results of those investigations should always be reported to the crisis team who can decide on action. Most experts agree that high-profile prosecutions and high-level publicity is the most effective action. The crisis team should prepare, in advance, detailed responses to media questions about how the company allowed the incident to happen and what measures are in place to prevent a recurrence.

CREDIT CONTROL FRAUD

Auditors should be on the look-out for instances of customers defaulting on debts and asking your company or organization to write off what is owed as a 'bad debt'. Such instances may be genuine defaults but may also be frauds being perpetrated against your company. Again, a decision has to be made whether to deal with it internally, externally or by both means.

ESPIONAGE

Espionage is a growing problem, not least because there is some evidence that the security services of some governments have turned away from spying in the recognized fashion and brought their expertise to bear on private companies. This often includes firms who are engaged in strategically important trading such as military equipment, aviation or major international projects.

One of the roles of the crisis team is to analyse what areas of the company's activities could be vulnerable to scrutiny by competitors or government agencies and engage expert advice on how to deal with it.

An important part of employee training is to emphasize the need for security at all times but particularly if they are working on sensitive situations or contracts. Indiscreet conversations on aircraft journeys can be just as damaging as having agents go through your unshredded rubbish.

ORGANIZED CRIME

A well-prepared crisis team will make an assessment of the company's vulnerability to the activities of organized crime gangs. Such gangs set up front companies and often instigate phoney commercial disputes involving huge sums of compensation to intimidate the innocent. They often act as if they are beyond the law and are often implicated in counterfeiting and kidnap plots. Once you have identified an actual or potential threat of this kind, you must make sure it is dealt with by experts.

It will truly become a crisis if you ignore it in the hope that the threat will go away or if you attempt to hide it under the carpet.

FORGERY

There are endless possibilities for forgery within a company or organization. Like so much else in this area, it is the responsibility of the financial controllers and auditors to watch out for altered documents and constantly monitor the credibility of documents' content. They also need to introduce methods of making sure that all internal documents are treated in such a way that they cannot be interfered with – for example, by using a secret marking or coding system.

BRIBERY

Definitions of bribery vary, but amount to the following: money or other inducements that persuade someone to act in favour of the giver. Bribes may include:

- gifts
- favours (for example, air mile awards)
- promises of employment
- threats of violence
- holiday visits disguised as business missions
- special arrangements for credit.

BLACKMAIL

For a crisis team there is no real alternative to taking a tough line against blackmail from the earliest possible moment. If a blackmailer thinks that a company is acting on its own, the consequences can be disastrous. The most important thing is to keep the blackmailer unaware that, or undecided whether, you have brought in the police. In reality, the police must be involved at the earliest possible stage and, as with incidents of terrorism or espionage, you must trust them and their methods of dealing with the crisis.

COMMISSION FIDDLES

Auditors and accountants must watch for the reliability of the calculation methods used by agents, salespeople and others whose income is derived from earning a percentage of the value of a contract.

However, this is an area in which there can be genuine misunderstandings and interpretations. Rather than immediately going outside for adjudication, it is often better to have an in-house procedure for resolving any arguments.

DUPLICATE INVOICES

Accounts departments must have a procedure for logging and tracking the approval process and a payment system for paying invoices. Suppliers may try to duplicate invoices if they think that the client systems are faulty. Automatic bank transfers have helped a great deal in this respect by flagging and tagging suppliers who appear to be attempting double or even triple payments.

EX-EMPLOYEE FRAUD

Corporate fraud is often perpetrated by employees who have left the company or organization but who still have an intimate knowledge of how it operates. Auditors should look out, in particular, for ex-employees who suddenly appear on the organization's list of vendors, often relying on friends who have subsequently joined the purchasing or other departments that commission work.

Another fraudulent activity often perpetrated by people who know that they are going to leave the company either of their own accord or at the company's instigation, is to take with them lists of the company's existing or potential clients. A check should be made for this when an employee leaves the staff.

EXTORTION

There are, potentially, more than a hundred ways in which an unscrupulous employee, former employee or aggrieved individual can hold an organization to ransom. Most common is probably product tampering accompanied by the threat that this will continue until money or another reward is paid. Another possibility is that sabotage may be threatened but not actually carried out, although this is still extortion and, as such, a serious crime. The same applies to threats to disable software or process systems.

As with many incidents involving crime, the sooner the police and other authorities are alerted the better. When appropriate, employees should be told about how the company acted in the hope that it will deter others in the future.

INSIDER DEALING

Broadly, insider dealing is the use of confidential information to influence the share price of a quoted company for personal gain. The information is usually to do with financial performance, company strategy and mergers and acquisitions. But it is a tricky area and there are many 'grey' situations where it is difficult to prove that insider dealing has actually taken place.

In the UK there have been relatively few prosecutions over the years despite (or perhaps because) the wide range of regulation on the issue. From the Stock Exchange through professional bodies and in the Bank of England there are procedures in place to try to spot the unusual movement of share prices.

Privately, most experts believe that the situation is still open to widespread abuse and that the regulators lack teeth. The Securities and Exchange Commission in the United States, however, is upheld as a model of toughness.

In crisis terms, all departments should be on the look-out for individuals who may be benefiting from their inside knowledge, and contractors of all sorts should be required to sign confidentiality agreements to prevent them from influencing the investment market. This is particularly true during so-called 'closed periods' when publicly quoted companies are not allowed to say certain things that may affect their share prices.

TERRORISM

As with sabotage, espionage and extortion, the earlier the outside agencies are called in to deal with potential or actual terrorist threats the better. Many companies employ former Special Branch or security experts to help prevent exposure to terrorists but when an act of terrorism actually occurs the official authorities must be advised immediately. There should be extensive staff training at all levels to make sure that terrorist activity is spotted and addressed. Almost all companies and organizations should expect to attract terrorist attention even if it only seems to be a remote possibility.

Of course, terrorism these days not only includes political actions (Irish and Middle East groups in particular) but single-issue action groups (animal rights groups, anti-Capitalism groups and so on).

TAX EVASION

A whole book could be devoted to this subject alone but, broadly speaking, this can impact as a crisis if auditors and accountants let it go undetected. Most tax evasion begins by accident but then becomes habitual if it is not rooted out.

Tax authorities are particularly tenacious when they have detected evasion and will demand immediate audits and compliance. They are also likely to revisit the issue in years to come. Employee tax evasion is a matter for the individual concerned, but it often involves the company in fraudulent claims and their problem can become yours if you fail to deal with it adequately.

COMPUTER HACKING

This is only one of many ways to commit computer crime. Its main elements are:

- accessing systems when you are not authorized to do so
- manipulating the records to create a false picture
- converting the false information to your advantage.

Any company with networked software systems should have reliable security methods (firewalls) to prevent illegal access, and these must be updated at regular intervals. Hacking is rarely an activity aimed at financially penalizing the company or organization. It is usually undertaken as a challenge by computer fanatics who want to prove that they can beat the system. Whatever form the hacking takes, it constitutes a crisis for most organizations, particularly those such as banks and insurance companies that advertise the security of their systems for the benefit of customers.

WIRE TRANSFER FRAUD

All companies should have systems, both internal and external, that do nothing else but protect the integrity of IT systems. This is particularly true of companies which transfer funds via the banking system.

In addition to implementing internal procedures for detecting irregularities, your crisis team would do well to make sure that the systems are evaluated by European and American Technology Security protocols. External consultants can be hired on a retainer basis or project to make sure that you and your customers are protected.

One bank we know of hired the computer experts who monitor the UK Ministry of Defence systems to sign off their software security. Apart from anything else, this was an excellent marketing tool.

REFERENCE

Comer, Michael J. (1998), *Corporate Fraud*, Aldershot; Gower.

Appendix 11: Call centres

CALL CENTRE CHECKLIST

Have we considered at least three different offerings?

Do they appear professional and reliable?

Have we visited them?

What recruitment and training policy have they?

Do they appear overloaded?

Are they willing to sign confidentiality agreements?

Do they appear to be familiar with your business?

Are they prepared to study your potential issues?

Do they offer a 24-hour service?

Have you tested their service anonymously?

Can they categorize types of call – for example, media versus customers/suppliers and so on?

Appendix 12: Community groups

COMMUNITY GROUPS CHECKLIST

Have we identified all the community groups that we need to keep in contact with?

Have staff been nominated to deal with each group?

Do we regularly invite community groups to social/business events?

Have we provided them with hotline numbers, and do these numbers work?

Are we prepared to do public service announcements and broadcasts in the event of a crisis?

Have we identified the key players (both positive and negative) in each group?

Index

accidents and disasters
  actions
    immediate 150–51
    later 151
  categories 149–50
accounting, false
  checking 137
  see also fraud
Agence France-Presse 49
Allied Domecq crisis
  background 80–81
  failure factors 81
ambulance service, Major Civil
    Emergency Plan 142–3
animal rights activism 26, 66–8, 139
appraisal systems, employees'
    concerns 36
Associated Press 49
Association of Professional Political
    Consultants 71
audiences
  importance 41–2
  internal 93–5
    learning points 95
  key, identification 13–14, 42
  learning points 18–19

Barings Bank crisis
  background 81–2
  failure factors 82
BBC, Programme Complaints Unit 135
Bhopal explosion 16
blackmail 162

Blair, Tony 83
BMW company 28
Brent Spar issue
  Greenpeace 32, 65–6
  Shell 32–3, 65–6
bribery 162
British Airports Authority,
    information gathering 84
British Biotech crisis 109–11
  'whistle-blower' 109–10
British Red Cross, Major Civil
    Emergency Plan 148
broadcasters
  complaints against 132–4
  regulation of 132
Broadcasting Standards Commission 133, 134–5
BSE, and the Conservative Party 14–15
bulletin boards, employees' concerns 35–6
'bulletin' story 50

call centres, checklist 167
campaign groups, environmental
    issues 31
Campbell, Alistair 83
caring agencies, Major Civil
    Emergency Plan 148
case studies
  Allied Domecq 80–81
  animal rights 66–8
  Barings Bank 81–2
  Brent Spar issue 65–6

171

INDEX

British Airports Authority 84
British Biotech crisis 109–11
Channel Tunnel fire 22–3
Coca-Cola, Belgium (1999) 17–18
Conservative Party and BSE 14–15
the disabled 68–9
Exxon Valdez crisis 77–9
Marchioness disaster 152–3
Monsanto and GM food 79–80
NATO, Kosovo crisis 83
Pepsi Cola, US 18
Townsend Thorensen 14
Victoria Station train 40–41
chairperson
  crisis team
    duties 115
    role 101–2
  deputy, crisis team
    duties 115
    role 102
Channel Tunnel fire 22–3
Clark, Wesley, Gen 83
clergy, Major Civil Emergency Plan 148
Coca-Cola, Belgium (1999) 17–18
Commercial Union Insurance, crisis management plan 16–17
commission fiddles 162
communications
  crisis management 9
  internal 93–5
  learning points 44
  member, crisis team
    duties 117
    role 103
  verbal 41
community groups, checklist 169
Compassion in World Farming 67
complaints
  against broadcasters 132–4
  against the media 131–5
  against newspapers 131–2
  authorities 134–5
computer hacking 165
Conservative Party, and BSE 14–15
councils, Major Civil Emergency Plan 144–5
counterfeiting 160–61

county chief executive, Major Civil Emergency Plan 145
county councils, lobbying 72–4
county supplies office, Major Civil Emergency Plan 147
county surveyors department, Major Civil Emergency Plan 146–7
county treasurers department, Major Civil Emergency Plan 147
credit control fraud 161
crime
  external 158–65
  internal 157–8
  organized 161
crisis
  audiences 13–14
  database 97–8
  defences 99
  definition 3
  emergency services 21–2, 24
  emotion vs logic 39–40
  financial, third-party endorsees 29–30
  financial consequences 15
  human resources implications 108
  identifying 35–6
  learning points 6, 37–8
  media coverage, stages 152
  media involvement 14
  medical issues 24–6
  new features 11
  post-crisis review 100
  preparation 87–91
    learning points 91
  recovery 10
  routines 48–9
  and share price 3–4
  simmering 3, 4, 6
  sudden 3, 4, 6
  see also emergencies
crisis centre 90
  checklist 119
crisis management
  advisers 90
  crisis communications 9
  crisis recovery 10
  critics, engagement with 25–6
  elements 7–12

emergency
  notification 8–9
  preparedness 7–8
  learning points 12
  priorities 4–5
  proactivity 36–7, 107
  security guards, role 89–90
  simulation 90–91
  see also crisis planning; crisis team
crisis planning 4
  Commercial Union Insurance 16–17
  crime
    external 158–65
    internal 157–8
  information technology, checklist 137–8, 154
  learning points 112
  plan, distribution 94
  telecommunications failure, checklist 155
  violence, threats of 153–4
  'what if' scenarios 107–8
  and the World Wide Web 139–40
crisis team 13
  action 105, 111
  agenda, typical 118
  chairperson 101–2, 115
    deputy 102, 115
  communications member 103, 117
  composition 88, 101–3
  duties 115–18
  environmental issues member 103
  finance member 102, 116
  follow-up 105
  health and safety member 103, 117
  human resources member 102, 116
  implementation 104
  learning points 106
  legal/insurance member 102, 116
  operations member 103, 117
  practice 104–5
  preparation 104
  question-and-answer document 88–9
  record-keeper 103, 118
  roles 87, 103–5

scope 88
critics, engagement with 25–6
customers, interests 27

database, crisis 97–8
deadlines 47–9
disabled activism 68–9
disasters *see* accidents and disasters

e-mail, checking 137
Ecclestone, Bernie 75
education department, Major Civil Emergency Plan 147
emergencies
  notification 8–9
  preparation 10–12
  preparedness 7–8
  sudden, list 5
  see also crisis
emergency services 21–2, 24
employees
  concerns
    appraisal systems 36
    bulletin boards 35–6
    channels 35–6
    newsletters 35
    suggestion boxes 36
    union representatives 36
  crisis plan details 94–5
Enron Corporation 159
environmental issues
  campaign groups 31
  crisis team 103
  third-party endorsees 31–3
espionage 161
extortion 163
Exxon Valdez crisis 16
  background 77–8
  failure factors 78–9

finance member, crisis team
  duties 116
  role 102
Financial Services Authority 82
fire and rescue service, Major Civil Emergency Plan 142
'flash' story 50
Flixborough explosion 31

173

INDEX

forgery 162
fraud
  corporate 157–65
  credit control 161
  ex-employee 163
  wire transfer 165
'Fresh Fish Test' 43–4
Friends of the Earth 31

Guiliani, Rudi 11
Green movements 31
Greenbury, Richard, Sir 30
Greenpeace, Brent Spar issue 32, 65–6

hacking
  checking 137
  computer 165
Hampshire, Major Civil Emergency Plan 141–8
hazards, potential, checklist 107
health authority/public health, Major Civil Emergency Plan 143–4
health and safety member, crisis team
  duties 117
  role 103
Hogg, Christopher, Sir 80–81
human resources
  crisis, implications 108
  member, crisis team
    duties 116
    role 102

Independent Television Commission 135
information technology, crisis planning, checklist 137–8, 154
inquiry log 98
  sample 123–4
insider dealing 163–4
Institute of Crisis Management 4
Internet
  misuse 138
  monitoring 139–40
    checklist 140
interviews, radio, advice 57–8
investigative programmes 61

invoices, duplicate 163

journalists
  background 46
  motivation 46, 48
  pack mentality 45
  trade press 52

Knight, Rory 15

Leeson, Nick 82
legal/insurance member, crisis team
  duties 116
  role 102
Lerbinger, Otto 5
lobby groups *see* single-issue lobby groups
lobbying
  county councils 72–4
  learning points 76
  local councils 72
  MEPs 74
  MPs 74
  parliamentary 74–6
  principles 71–2
  see also single issue lobby groups
local councils, lobbying 72
Lockerbie air disaster (1988) 16

McDonalds, attacks by PETA 139
Major Civil Emergency Plan 73–4
  ambulance service 142–3
  British Red Cross 148
  caring agencies 148
  clergy 148
  councils 144–5
  county chief executive 145
  county supplies office 147
  county surveyors department 146–7
  county treasurers department 147
  education department 147
  estates 145
  fire and rescue service 142
  Hampshire 141–8
  health authority/public health 143–4
  police 141

INDEX

property 145
St John Ambulance 148
scientific services 145–6
social services department 146
trading standards 146
Women's Royal Voluntary Service 147–8
Major, John 66
Marchioness disaster, media coverage 152–3
Marks and Spencer, third-party endorsees 30
Maxwell, Robert, pension scandal 29
media
  complaints against 131–5
  coverage
    Marchioness disaster 152–3
    stages 152
media handling
  checklist 127–8
  learning points 62
  log, sample 128–9
medical issues 24–6
MEPs, lobbying 74
messages, key 42–4
Metropolitan Police (London) 152
Mirror Group pensioners 29
Monsanto, GM food
  background 79
  failure factors 80
MPs, lobbying 74

National Institute for Clinical Excellence (NICE) 25
NATO, Kosovo crisis, media elements 83
Neill Commission, Standards in Public Life 75
Nestlé company 25
new technologies 60–61
news
  conferences, checklist 122–3
  items, structure 46
  priority ratings 50
news agencies
  accessibility 51
  main companies 49
  news classification 50

newsletters, employees' concerns 35
newspapers
  complaints against 131–2
  local 56
  mid-market tabloids 53–4
  quality broadsheets 53
  'red tops' 54–5
  regional 55–6
NICE *see* National Institute for Clinical Excellence

operations member, crisis team
  duties 117
  role 103
overcharging 16

Pan-Am flight 103
  Lockerbie 16
parallel trading 160
Parliament, lobbying 74–6
Pepsi Cola, US 18
PETA (People for the Ethical Treatment of Animals), vs McDonalds 139
phone-in programmes 57–8
planning *see* crisis planning
police, Major Civil Emergency Plan 141
'Ponzi' scheme 159
Press Agency (PA) 50
Press Complaints Commission 134
Press Council 134
Pretty, Deborah 15
price-fixing 158–9
proactivity, crisis management 36–7, 107
product recall, third-party endorsees 26–7
product tampering 154
  third-party endorsees 27
Public Interest Disclosure Act (1998) 36, 93
pyramid schemes 159

question-and-answer document 88–9

radio
  growth 56–7

INDEX

interviews, advice 57–8
   phone-in programmes 57–8
Radio Authority 135
RAF, 'whistle-blowers' 111
Rainbow Warrior 65
record-keeper, crisis team
   duties 118
   role 103
'red top' tabloids 54–5
redundancies, third-party endorsees 27–8
Reuters 49
risks, review of 37
Rover Group 28
Royal Family, and the tabloids 55
'Rule of Five' 44

St John Ambulance, Major Civil Emergency Plan 148
scientific services, Major Civil Emergency Plan 145–6
Securities and Exchange Commission (US) 164
security guards, crisis management role 89–90
September 11 (2001) attack 11
share price, and crisis 3–4
Shea, Jamie 83
Shell, Brent Spar issue 32–3, 65–6
Sierra Club 31
simulation, crisis management 90–91
single-issue lobby groups (SILO)
   dealing with 64–5
   examples 65–9
   learning points 69
   origins 63
'snap' story 50
social services department, Major Civil Emergency Plan 146
'spin-doctoring' 42
spokesperson 97–100
   advice 122
   duties 121
   learning points 100
staff *see* employees
stakeholders 13, 14
suggestion boxes, employees' concerns 36

tabloid newspapers
   categories 53–5
   political allegiance 55
   and the Royal Family 55
Tass news agency 49
tax evasion 164
telecommunications failure, checklist 155
television interviews
   advice 58–60
   live 60
terrorism 164
Thatcher, Margaret 57–8
third-party endorsees 21, 26
   environmental issues 31–3
   financial crisis 29–30
   learning points 33
   Marks and Spencer 30
   product recall 26–7
   product tampering 27
   redundancies 27–8
Three Mile Island accident 31
tobacco advertising 75
Townsend Thoresen 14
trade press 51–2
trading standards, Major Civil Emergency Plan 146
training 125

Union Carbide, Bhopal explosion 16
union representatives, employees' concerns 36

Victoria Station, train accident 40–41
visual aids, impact 43

wash-up, post-crisis 100
'what if' scenarios, crisis planning 107–8
'whistle-blowers'
   British Biotech 109–10
   protection 36, 93–4, 111
   RAF 111
wire services *see* news agencies
Women's Royal Voluntary Service, Major Civil Emergency Plan 147–8

Zeebrugge tragedy 14

If you have found this book useful you may be interested in other titles from Gower

Corporate Fraud 3ed
Michael J. Comer
0 566 07810 4

Investigating Corporate Fraud
Michael J. Comer
0 566 08531 3

Statistical Sampling and Risk Analysis in Auditing
Peter Jones
0 566 08080 X

Managing Communications in a Crisis
Peter Ruff and Khalid Aziz
0 566 08294 2

How to Keep Operating in a Crisis: Managing a Business in a Major Catastrophe
James Callan
0 566 08523 2

Fire Precautions: A Guide for Management
Colin S. Todd
0 566 08182 2

Security Manual 7ed
John Wilson and David Brooksbank
0 566 08174 1

GOWER